MARS ATTACKS
MEMOIRS

ALSO BY JONATHAN GEMS

FICTION

Mars Attacks!
(published by Penguin)

NON-FICTION

Who Killed British Cinema?
(with Vinod Mahindru)

PLAYS

Santa Rides Out
The Shithouse of the August Moon
Rinni Bootsie Tutti Frutti
The Tax Exile
Back to Nature
The Secret of the Universe
Naked Robots
Doom, Doom, Doom, Doom
The Paranormalist
Susan's Breasts

FILMS

Nineteen Eighty-Four
White Mischief
Mars Attacks!
The Treat

MARS ATTACKS
MEMOIRS

INTERVIEWS WITH SCREENWRITER
JONATHAN GEMS
BY MILA POP

Q

QUOTA BOOKS LTD

First published in Great Britain 2020

QUOTA BOOKS LTD

The Studio, 197 Hammersmith Grove, London w6 onp

The rights of Mila Pop and Jonathan Gems to be identified as the Authors of the Work have been asserted by them in accordance with Section 7 of the Copyright, Designs and Patents Act 1988.

ISBN 978-1-9162460-3-4

Quota Books is fully committed to a sustainable, low carbon emissions future, in accordance with the United Nations' agenda for sustainable development and global domination. We use approved materials that are natural, renewable, recyclable, and sustainable from wood grown in forests that conform to international logging and environmental standards, and are processed in accordance with the American National Standard for Information Sciences – Permanence of Paper for Printed Library Materials (ANSI Z39.48-1992)

www.quotabooks.com

Typeset and text design by Tetragon, London
Printed and bound by Biddles
Cover by: Tristan

FOR LISA-MARIE SMITH

The following is an edited transcript of a series of interviews I conducted with Jonathan Gems between November 2019 and February 2020.

I believe this will be of interest to fans of the movie, and also to those interested in Hollywood and filmmaking in general.

—MILA POP

INTRODUCTION

Jonathan opened the door and led me through the house and out, down some steps, into a back garden to the old painter's studio where he worked – a little sanctuary in the middle of London. The studio looks like a mix between a library and child's playroom, with walls lined with books, several desks and tables, and a daybed. It was so quiet, I didn't feel like I was in Shepherd's Bush. All I could hear was birdsong.

As I set up my recording equipment, he offered me a drink, and began talking about the times he'd had with the people on the movie. I'd known Jonathan a long time and thought it would be a good idea to interview him about his experiences working on *Mars Attacks!*

While he was having his Yorkshire tea, I was sipping coffee, and preparing my questions. Excitement was in the air! We were going to uncover the story behind this amazing, crazy, and great movie whose fans continue to grow after almost a quarter of a century. The movie with a huge cast of stars helmed by one of Hollywood's greatest directors, Tim Burton.

And this was a great opportunity to peek into the world of filmmaking from the screenwriter's point of view.

—MILA POP

INTERVIEW 1

MP: Okay, *Mars Attacks!* So, how did it start?

JG: Well, I think it was 1994. It was in the summer, and I was walking down Melrose Avenue in Los Angeles, looking for a present for Tim Burton's birthday. I went into this gift shop, and was looking around, and I found these cards. There were two sets. You could buy the whole set. They were like baseball cards, or cigarette cards. Kids used to buy candy cigarettes or gum and collect the cards and swap them.

Anyway, these cards were called *Mars Attacks!* and there was another set of cards called *Dinosaurs Attack!* – and I was looking at these cards and thinking: Wow! These were beautiful little images of sadistic-looking Martians killing everything, and I thought they were great. So, it was an impulse buy. I bought a set of *Mars Attacks!* cards and a set of *Dinosaurs Attack!* Got them both. I thought they were fun.

MP: Is it because Tim Burton was a cartoonist before? That's why you thought he'd like these cards?

JG: Well, not exactly. But Tim's an artist. He's a visual artist, and I thought he might respond to these cards. I was a visual artist as well at one time. I went to art school. I was a painter and I used to do cartoons. I liked the cards so I thought he might like them too. We were both into the same kind of stuff. You know, we both read the same horror comics when we were kids, which is probably why we're so screwed up. Ha ha.

So, I got Tim these two sets of baseball cards as a birthday present 'cause what can you get for Tim Burton? He didn't really need anything. I just wanted to get him something amusing. So, that's what I got him. And he was delighted by them. He thought they were great.

MP: Such kids, you two, huh? Little boys, but working in such a serious world.

JG: I suppose. And I think both Tim and myself are sometimes inclined to get depressed. So, little things like those cards, that maybe seem trivial to some people, are quite important, in a way, because they cheer us up. Anyway, he was looking at these cards and he had an idea.

He said: "Let's do a movie based on the *Dinosaurs Attack!* cards." He liked that one. He liked the other one too, but he liked that one better. Because they were great little pictures of dinosaurs walking around Los Angeles, killing everybody.

So, we talked about that. And then we realized we couldn't do it because of *Jurassic Park*. Steven Spielberg had done a movie with dinosaurs killing people. And there were rumors, at that time, that he was gonna do *Jurassic Park* #2, with dinosaurs coming to Los Angeles.

So, Tim was kind of ruffling his hair, and thinking about this, and then he said: "I've got to make up my mind what my next picture's gonna be." He said he had four or five possibilities, but he had to make up his mind by the end of the month. Then he said: "I can't do *Dinosaurs Attack!* but if you can come up with a treatment for *Mars Attacks!* – something I can show the studio – that might be another option."

It was a long shot, and I wasn't getting paid and, right off the bat, I didn't have an idea how to do it. So, I said to Tim: "What kind of movie should it be?" And he said: "A disaster movie, like Irwin Allen. Like *The Towering Inferno*."

Well, my eyes lit up. I saw it immediately. A big cast of dopey characters running around being chased by these horrible-looking Martians. It was funny. So, I said: "Cool! I'll do it!"

And he said: "Let's watch The Towering Inferno." So, we went to Rocket Video on Highland Avenue, and rented *The Towering Inferno*, and went to his house to watch it. And it was really funny. There's a scene where Robert Wagner falls out through the window, at the top of the burning skyscraper, in a ball of flame. Tim thought it was hilarious. We both did.

You see, it was unexpected. Robert Wagner was this very good-looking star, and you don't do that to a star. Not in a Hollywood movie. Not in any kind of movie. You don't kill the star, unless it's the villain. Only the small-part actors get killed. It's a golden rule. So, it's kind of shocking when you see it. And it's funny.

After seeing that, it all came to me fairly quickly. And, in about a week, I had it roughed out: the story and the characters. And when I finished it, I realized it was inevitably going to be – it couldn't help being – a portrait of America because, following the Irwin Allen formula, I'd sketched out a range of different characters from different walks of life, and placed the action in different locations – in this case: California, Nevada, Kansas, New York, Mount Rushmore, and Washington D.C.

And the Martians on the cards were grotesque. They were extreme. So that set the bar. It meant the human characters had to be somewhat extreme too. They had to be heightened. I was in the realm of satire and comedy. And I remembered a funny play I'd seen called *Bartholomew Fair*, by Ben Jonson, which was... Well, it has a large cast, and was a kind of satirical portrait of London. So, I got ahold of a copy of the play, and read it. And I also watched *It's a Mad, Mad, Mad, Mad World*, with Spencer Tracy, Ethel Merman, Milton Berle and all those guys, which is a wonderful portrait of American society written by Bill Rose, one my most favorite screenwriters. And, while I was figuring out the story, I thought that, rather than having just one of the stars die, like in *The Towering Inferno*, *all* the stars would die. And this led to the concept that, in this movie at least, the lesser-known actors would wind up being the heroes. So, that was how the theme developed.

MP: So, what is the theme of *Mars Attacks!*?

JG: Well, it's: "Don't trust the experts."

MP: Oh yes!

JG: Is that the theme or is that the message? I'm not quite sure. Anyway, I was writing a comedy. And comedies have happy endings, right? So, I couldn't have the Martians win. Someone had to save the world. And it would be so boring if it was the usual dumb big man on campus played by a star. So, it had to be a lesser-known actor playing someone insignificant in the story. So, that's why I came up with the idea of an unloved boy and his neglected grandmother who save the world.

MP: Wow.

JG: And that led to the idea that, in this case, the authorities are wrong about everything. All the authority figures, who are played by stars, are out of their depth. They can't handle it. And as I was writing this – sketching it out really – it felt liberating. I could feel it was going to be liberating.

So anyway, I wrote the treatment, which is just another word for the story. It took about a week. And then I went over to see Tim. Went over to his house. And he read it while I sat there. I was nervous, very nervous, because what I'd written was still kind of rough, and I hadn't... There was one major element I hadn't figured out. I'd tried and tried, but I just couldn't think of anything. It was how the boy and his granny defeat the Martians. I didn't have a clue how they would do it.

Anyway, after Tim read the treatment, he was frowning, like he didn't like it. And I started talking – I couldn't stop talking – about the story, the characters, why I did it this way and that way and how it could work and everything. And he just kept frowning harder and harder. And when I finished talking, he said: "How do they defeat the Martians? It's not in there."

So, I confessed that I didn't know. I'd been bashing my brains over it, but it was really hard to come up with an idea because the Martians were so advanced. You know, nuclear weapons were like pea-shooters to them, and they had all these robots and ray-guns and spaceships and everything.

And, like it was nothing, Tim said: "Well, why not music?"

MP: Hahaha! But you see, the two of you together, there's such a connection. You inspire each other. It's not like you're bashing your brains, and he comes up with it like it's nothing. You're bouncing off each other. You were working hard on it, and you come up with all these ideas, and that sparks ideas in him.

JG: Yeah, well, that's why I like working with him. He's very creative. I mean, I hadn't had a lot of experience with directors. I'd only worked on three films before. But I'd worked with a lot of stage directors and, to be honest, none of them were… Well, in a sense you might call them creative, but none of them were like Tim Burton. Not remotely. It's an extraordinary pleasure to work with an artist like Tim. It's a lot of fun. And his taste is very good, so you feel safe with him.

MP: And of course, he does a different kind of work. But then you do the hard work of writing. I would imagine for him it's great when someone puts this big structure together. And for you it's great to have him because he's also an artist and can enhance what you're doing.

JG: Yeah, that's right. I mean, he came up with things I never would have thought of. He's really imaginative. Things that just blew me away. But they fit right into it, and they made the film so much better. Like…

MP: It's like a band.

JG: Yeah, like a band. It's like having a great lead singer. That's what's so good about filmmaking. If you're working with really talented people, it's wonderful. And, so yeah, he would come up with ideas. He came up with the idea of music killing the Martians. And we brainstormed different death scenes for the stars. So, for example, Glenn Close, who played the First Lady. He thought it would be fun to have a big, heavy chandelier come down on top of her. And I came up with the line: "Oh no! The Nancy Reagan chandelier!"

It was fun devising all the death scenes. But I couldn't come up with a good way to kill the president. He was the most prominent character in the film, later played by Jack Nicholson, so he needed a spectacular death. His death, which was almost the last one, had to top all the others.

So, like with my 'how to kill the Martians' problem, I said to Tim: "I don't know how to kill the president. I can't think of anything that's gonna top what we've done before."

And Tim was really thinking about this. He really had his thinking cap on. And it took him a few days. And then, I was staying... He had this house, a magical house, in Ojai, about seventy miles outside of Los Angeles. The house was on top of a hill. There's a whole story about that house I'll tell you later.

Anyway, I was staying there, writing the script, and Tim and Lisa-Marie were there, and it was a lovely place to write. Very peaceful. The weather was perfect. I did some of the writing under a tree out by the pool. Lisa-Marie would come and bring me snacks, and glasses of iced tea. She was so beautiful. I was in love with her and Tim both. But I didn't know how to kill the president.

Then, about three days after I'd dropped the problem in his lap, Tim came into this little study room where I was typing. I think it was in the morning. I was in this little alcove room, and he came in, and he said: "How about this?" And he had some drawings in his hand.

See, the Martians had conquered America, and the Martian Commander marches into the Oval Office with his squad, and confronts the president. Well, I'd written this speech for the president, this dumb political speech where he says: "Why can't we just get along? Earth and Mars, together?" And the Martian Commander is moved by this corny speech, and gets a tear in his eye.

Then Tim said: "How about this?" And he outlined, with illustrations, what you see in the movie. You know, the Martian Commander steps forward and puts out his hand. He wants to shake hands with the president. The president is nervous, of course, but starting to hope that everything's gonna be fine. The war's over. There's going to be peace. So, he gingerly shakes the Martian Commander's hand. But then the hand of the Martian Commander detaches itself from his wrist, and crawls up the president's arm like a scorpion. It goes over his shoulder and scuttles down his back. And the president's thinking: "What the hell's going on here?" And then the finger turns into a spike and stabs him through the back, right through his body, and out through his chest. And shocked, the president falls to the ground, pierced through the heart. Then the finger extends like a telescope, and the top of the spike opens, and out comes the Martian flag!

MP: It's just brilliant!

JG: I was like: "Oh, my God, how did you think of that? That's incredible! Thanks Tim, you've solved it!"

And then he said: "Yeah, but I don't know what should be on the flag."

So, now he got me thinking about the flag. So, we both were sketching different designs and, for some reason, the dollar bill popped into my head. You know, the pyramid with the eye. I didn't know how this fit into the overall theme of the movie, but it felt as if equating the Martians with money said something. And, later, as the screenplay evolved, I realized what it was. The theme wasn't only 'Don't trust the experts,' it was a tilt at all the things in society that oppress us – and money is one of those things.

But at the time I wasn't thinking that. I just liked the image of the eye in the pyramid because it was spooky. It reminded me of the All-Seeing Eye of Agamotto in the *Doctor Strange* comics – the ones drawn by Steve Ditko – who created this great, spooky sci-fi atmosphere, which kind of fit with the scary world of the Martians.

Anyway, Tim looked at it and he said: "Well, yeah, maybe something like that." And he began sketching it a bunch of different ways – trying out different, more abstract styles. And then he settled on one of them. Um, I can't remember now but it was like a pink triangle and with an eye in it. And that's what he used in the film. And we didn't think much of it at the time. It was just an image. It didn't mean anything...

MP: At the time?

JG: Yeah. It wasn't until, a dozen years later, that I found out, I think it was on Alex Jones, his website *Infowars*, that this was similar to the Illuminati flag. I mean, we didn't know about the Illuminati back then. This was in 1995. Before the Internet got going; before laptops. I was writing the script on yellow legal pads, and then typing it up on an electric typewriter. And globalism, the central banking system, the New World Order, the Deep State – we didn't know about any of that. It wasn't known about. Very few people knew about it. That was like their flag, supposedly. But we had no knowledge of that. We weren't saying the Martians were bankers, or anything. It was an accident.

MP: It's amazing how the artists, just playing around, having ideas, put things together that, later on, mean something. It's like you're psychic or something.

JG: Well, I don't know about that...

MP: Because some people think you were writing about the Illuminati.

JG: We weren't. We didn't know anything about the Illuminati. We were just playing around. But, later, much later, I did wonder if maybe we'd offended some higher-ups. Because of what happened when the film was released.

MP: What happened when it was released?

JG: Well, the studio didn't really support it. They were negative about it. And there was no reason to be. It was a fun movie. It scored very high in the test screenings. The test screenings were a trip. The first one was in San Francisco. I had to fly up on the plane, and I was almost late. I got there as it started. And it was an extraordinary experience. It was held in this big movie theater. The place was packed with college kids. Tim was nervous. He was in the projection booth.

I got a seat in the audience; there were a lot of executives there, Warner Bros executives, sitting and standing at the back, and going in and out of the door. And Bob Daly, the president of Warner's, was there. Tim was hiding from them. And all these students from that college in San Francisco, Berkeley. They'd got free tickets in exchange for filling out a questionnaire, asking detailed questions, to get their thoughts about the movie. And this test screening was the first public screening. Tim wasn't happy about it because the movie wasn't finished. They'd stuck in a temp music track, and cards saying 'visual effect here,' and 'scene missing.' He hated people seeing the movie before it was finished. It was painful for him.

Anyway, the audience went *wild!* They went absolutely *nuts!* And, halfway through the movie, they started doing a thing I'd never seen before. Drumming their feet. Drumming their feet hard on the floor. It sounded like thunder. Hundreds of feet drumming on the floor. It was deafening! They were so excited and, at the end of the film, they all stood up, whooping and hollering.

It was extraordinary. The studio executives were bewildered by it. Despite the blanks in the film, and the animated sequences that weren't finished, the students totally loved the movie.

After it was over, I went out into the lobby, and noticed a huddle of Warner Bros executives. And Bob Daly, the president, saw me and said: "Hey, Jonathan, come over here." So, I went over and, it was strange, all the executives formed a line, like a line of men in Armani suits. Bob Daly was in the middle. And he said: "Where's Tim?"

I said: "He was in the projection booth. Do you want me to go find him?"

Daly shook his head and said: "Well, where is he? We're waiting for him."

He was annoyed that Tim was avoiding him. He was the boss of Warner Bros, after all, and I guess he felt he was being insulted.

So, I tried to smooth things over. "I'm sure he'll be out in a minute."

All the executives were tense. They were kind of sweating with tension. So, I tried to get them to chill out. I smiled at the president and said: "So, what did you think? It went well didn't it?" This was an understatement. I doubt if they'd ever seen such an ecstatic reaction to a movie. I know I never had. I mean, they had to be pleased by this amazing audience reaction. But Bob Daly was tight lipped. He didn't want to say anything. So, I turned to the executive next to him, and said: "What did you think? Did you like it?" But he kept his mouth shut too, and barely acknowledged me. I was mystified. Why were they so uptight? So, I turned back to the president. "Well, the audience liked it a lot, didn't they? That's a good sign. Don't you think?"

Very reluctantly, after a strained pause, Daly said: "It played great." And he made a chopping gesture with his hand. I turned to the guy on his right, who made the same chopping gesture, and said: "It played great." And then, all along the line, the executives made the same chopping gesture, and each one of them said: "It played great!"

If I hadn't seen it, I wouldn't have believed it. It was like an over-the-top parody of studio yes-men. But it really happened.

MP: None of them said what they thought of it?

JG: No! They all said it played great, which is saying nothing because, of course it played great. The audience was screaming with delight. Nobody could deny that.

There were some guys from Industrial Light & Magic there, so I went to talk to them, and a little while later, Tim emerged, and I saw Bob Daly and the executives pounce on him. It was like they swallowed him up. And I didn't see him after that.

The second test screening was a preview in, I think, Universal City Walk. It was a big, big movie theater, an invited audience, mostly teenagers, mostly students. And I went with a couple of friends, a couple of English friends, and I was looking forward to seeing it. I hadn't seen it with all the effects done and finished, and I couldn't wait to hear Danny Elfman's music.

So, now it was finished, completely finished, and we went in and it was a big audience, maybe six hundred people, and it took off like a rocket. Almost from the start, they were laughing and banging their feet on the floor and, like at the first screening, they cheered and whistled at the end. It was intense. Euphoric. They totally loved the movie and, when we came out, I was in a daze, and so were my friends.

It felt like we were on drugs. It was more like we'd been to a rock concert than a movie. I remember how grateful I was for the cool air, and that my friends were with me because I was so dazed and it was good knowing they were going to drive me home.

They couldn't stop talking about how amazing the movie was. They were gob-smacked. They were saying: "This is going to be *huuuge!* It's going to be *massive!* It's gonna break records!" And they were looking at me with a new expression. Looking at me almost like I was a stranger to them. It was a chilly feeling. It was like: "Is he gonna stay friends with us now?" And I got that de-stabilizing sensation I'd had before, when I had a hit play in London. I mean, we all want to be successful but, when it happens, it's alienating. It's gratifying in one way, but in another way, it's not pleasant. Not at all. It cuts you off from your friends. And people get envious. Success is good because it gives you opportunities to do the things you want to do. But, in many ways, failure is easier to handle. And the reaction of the audience worried me because it was so out of control. It was abnormal. It was like they were on laughing gas. And I didn't understand it. I couldn't see what they were seeing. I couldn't understand it.

MP: I loved it when I saw it.

JG: I don't know what I was expecting. I was just hoping it would work, that's all. I wasn't expecting this kind of over-the-top reaction. And I was worried by what my friends were saying because I was scared of being too successful. I didn't know what it would do to me.

But I needn't have worried because the studio didn't like it. No one from Warner Bros said anything complimentary about the film, despite the high test scores. And this was a big mystery to me. When I talked to my agent, Jeff Field, about it, he said they were waiting to see how it did on the opening weekend. They weren't going to waste their breath making compliments now. If the movie had a great opening weekend, then we'd get some compliments.

But I definitely sensed an icy wind coming from the studio, and this was born out in the release campaign, which was kind of half-assed. Some genius had come up with a tag line: "Nice Planet. We'll take it." Talk about lame! And it showed me they didn't understand the movie. It's not about the Martians. The posters and trailers made it about the Martians, when they were only the catalyst. The movie is about the people. They should have featured the cast – and we had a great cast – not the Martians. In my opinion, the marketing was terrible.

The trouble was the head of marketing had just left. And Warner Bros were looking for a replacement. The marketing people were leaderless and they weren't confident. They didn't know how to sell the film. And what was really frustrating was they wouldn't talk to me. They refused to talk to me. I could have helped them, but they wouldn't talk to me!

Once Tim had the idea of *Mars Attacks!* as a disaster movie, the marketing issue was solved. You sell it as a disaster movie. Like Irwin Allen sold *The Towering Inferno*. A big poster with photos of all the stars on it – looking worried.

But the marketing guys were running around like headless chickens. That was the problem. I'm sure the previous head of marketing – I wish I could remember his name! He was a genius. He was the man who did *Batman*, which was revolutionary, a game-changer. If he'd still been there, things would have been different. He must have been disgusted by the *Mars Attacks!* campaign.

MP: You know, we didn't hear much about *Mars Attacks!* when it came out. Except they showed the trailer on TV a few times.

JG: Right, right. Well, in L.A., I was waiting for the hype to start, and it didn't happen. Nothing was happening! And I started to panic. Tim was away in India, and the release date was three weeks away, and there was no publicity. Even *Entertainment Weekly*, which was the magazine which always covered the new releases and, normally, would have had three or four pages with pictures of *Mars Attacks!* did nothing. They didn't cover it at all!

I made lots of calls to Warner Bros and they gave me the runaround. And then, when I finally got through to someone, they said: "Oh, we're working hard on the campaign. We're spending ten million dollars on it." So, I went: "But where is it? I don't see anything!" Then, a week before the release, a billboard appeared on Sunset Boulevard, and they started showing the trailer in movie theaters. But it had no impact. It was very confusing. After the amazing test-screening results, I assumed they'd get behind the movie and do a lot of promotion. But it didn't happen. They showed some clips on TV, but they were too short and they weren't funny. We had a movie with an incredible cast. Twenty stars! But they only featured five of them! It was baffling.

About four months later, *The Fifth Element*, directed by Luc Besson, was released in an explosion of publicity. There were ads and teaser trailers, and lots of coverage in newspapers and magazines, and interviews on high-rated TV shows. And the trailers looked sexy and enticing. I remember thinking: "Why wasn't *Mars Attacks!*" publicized like this?"

The Fifth Element grossed about $64 million domestically, which was what *Mars Attacks!* should have done.

MP: Do you know they're still playing it in some cinemas in Paris?

JG: What, now?

MP: Yes. I just checked it online.

JG: Are you serious? They're still playing *Mars Attacks!*?

MP: Yes.

JG: Incredible. The French are weird.

MP: They love it!

JG: They also love Jerry Lewis movies.

MP: I know why they love *Mars Attacks!* It's because they're so freedom loving, and quirky, and they love everything weird. But it has to be intelligent to work in France. I mean, you can't have something weird for the sake of it.

JG: I can't believe they're still showing it.

MP: It sounds like you're saying the release campaign was deliberately bad.

JG: Yeah, I know. And that doesn't make sense, does it? It couldn't have been deliberately bad. They wouldn't deliberately sabotage their own product, would they? And even if they, or someone, put the word out to pan the movie, *Pee-wee's Big Adventure** got bad reviews, but it still did great business.

But, you know, studio politics is a funny thing. There was a faction at Warner's that wanted the movie to fail. You see, there were two guys competing for the job of Warner Bros president, and *Mars Attacks!* was the project of one of them. So, if it had been a big hit, that would have been a feather in his cap and maybe would have helped him get the job. But, if it was a flop, the other guy would get the job.

But I'll tell you one thing. While I was there, at Warner Bros, there was a big debate going on as to what was more important: the movie or the release campaign. And I'll tell you the answer. It's the release campaign. The release campaign is more important than the movie. If you have a great film with a lousy release, nobody will see it. But a lousy film with a great release, everybody will see it.

---

* Tim Burton's first feature film.

MP: Well, that's why now, after so many years, soooo many people love *Mars Attacks!* It's word of mouth.

JG: Word of mouth, yeah...

MP: I mean, even though it had a bad release, still, I mean, it went around the world... and people love it. You can't keep a good film down...

JG: Yes, and you have to give Warner Bros credit for making it. I've been a little negative about them but actually, without them, the movie would never have been made.

MP: Maybe another studio would have made it...

JG: Well, that is true, but... apart from the marketing, every-thing else was pretty successful. I mean, we were very lucky with the actors. And everybody worked very, very hard – the cast and the crew. And we were lucky with lots of things. Like the hotel in Las Vegas. The Landmark. Which they were blowing up, and we got to film it. And it was a great-looking hotel. It fit so well with the design of the movie, people thought it was a model. There were all sorts of lucky things like that that happened.

We did a recce in Vegas. And we visited this sign graveyard. A scrap-yard full of these great, old Vegas signs – custom-made signs – spelling out the names of hotels, or lounges, or casi-nos, or whatever. It was like a big scrap-yard full of these old Vegas signs. And I thought it was fantastic. So, when we got back, I wrote a scene set in this Vegas sign graveyard. And, later on, they let us shoot there.

MP: The scene with Danny DeVito?

JG: Yeah.

MP: I thought that was a set.

JG: Yeah, I know. It looks fake, doesn't it?

MP: Yeah.

JG: That happens a lot. The fake stuff looks real, and the real stuff looks fake. Haha!

MP: Oh wow!

JG: Haha, yeah. But we were very lucky. And Tim had a great team, like Colleen Atwood, the costume designer, Ve Neill, who supervised the make-up. She was the best. Very funny. And she was like a hen mother to the other make-up girls.

MP: Oh really?

JG: Yeah. She ruled the roost. And she was in love with Jack Nicholson. Very smart and funny. They were a very nice bunch of people. We had very nice people working on the film. Chris Lebenzon, the editor, was very nice...

MP: What's happened to the kids now?

JG: What kids?

MP: You know, the black kids that save the president, and play video games instead of going to school.

JG: Oh, them! Haha. Weren't they nice? Good casting. I don't know. I'll tell you this, though. Tim was wonderful with them. He was absolutely fabulous with them.

MP: They were so sweet!

JG: Yeah. He was great with the kids. Because, you see, I saw Tim working on *Batman*, and I'd seen him on other films. Um, and he didn't seem to direct the actors very much. And I'd come out of the theater, which is quite different. The director is constantly at it with the actors. And I'd worked on a couple of Mike Radford movies before, and Mike used to talk to the actors a lot too. You know, discussing what they were gonna do, how they were going to play it, and fine-tuning the performances. But Tim didn't do that. And I thought, well maybe this is an American thing?

But, when it came to the kids, he spent a lot of time with them. He was very, very warm and very kind. He relaxed them, and amused them, made them happy, and got them into a really good zone. I'm pretty sure they were amateurs or, at least, they hadn't done much film acting before. They were a little bit frightened by everything. But Tim gently and clearly explained what they had to do, and he made them feel good. And they did really well. They were perfect. He put a lot of time and attention into them. He didn't do that with the other actors because they didn't need it.

MP: I suppose, when you have such a good cast, you don't really need to tell them what to do.

JG: Not much. The main thing is to get out of their way. Unless they're going off-course. Then you might step in and say something.

MP: You let them do their thing.

JG: Exactly. It's their work, their skill, their art. You support them in what they're doing. You give them whatever they need. If they need help with something, usually they will ask you.

MP: Right. It's like trust.

JG: Yeah. You have to trust your actors. Very important. If you don't trust them, they feel it, and it undermines them.

MP: Also, I have noticed, when you let things... When you're doing something creative, and you are supposedly directing the process, the natural order of things starts happening. I've noticed that even if it becomes seemingly messy, something will happen, someone will freak out about it being messy, and things will start ordering themselves naturally.

JG: Yeah, that's right. Did I tell you about the opening weekend?

MP: The opening weekend?

JG: Yeah, see, when they release a film, they judge everything by the opening weekend.

MP: Yeah?

JG: Yeah. My agent, Jeff Field, called me – I think it was on Sunday. The opening weekend begins on a Friday, and they get the numbers in, you see? For Friday and then Saturday. I think it was Sunday he called me. And he said: "It's a flop." Because, for it to be a hit, it had to do, I think, $15 million and it did about $9 million. That meant it was a flop. And it also meant that the schedules for other releases were changed, and the run of the film was reduced to two to three weeks instead of four to six weeks. In Los Angeles, the run was only 17 days.

If we'd had an opening weekend of $15 million, they would have scheduled a six-week run in all the theaters in America. But because it was only $9 million, they cut that down to two weeks in most venues, so that limited the amount of people that could see it. And, of course, there was no time for word of mouth to grow.

And, by the end of the run, which was only three weeks, the film had grossed about $40 million, which wasn't bad, but not quite enough. We needed to gross $60 million. See, as a rule of thumb, for a film to be a hit, the worldwide gross has to be three times the production cost. So, the total gross needed to be $210 million. And the U.S. domestic gross was generally one quarter of the worldwide gross. So, they projected that the total gross would be four times $40 million. $160 million – which is a lot less than $210 million. Therefore, *Mars Attacks!* was a flop. Plus, we had bad reviews. We had a lot of reviews saying it was 'camp' and a waste of time.

But then what happened was, they released it in Europe, and the people doing the marketing and distribution were different people, and they did a better campaign, and the film was a hit. In Europe, it grossed roughly $120 million, I think. Something like that.

MP: Wow!

JG: And, with the revenues from other territories, such as Japan, South Korea, China, Australia, Canada – there are about thirty other territories – the movie grossed more than $210 million and was a hit.

MP: And then did they say: "This is a hit?"

JG: No, they didn't. It was strange. Some people were saying: "Hey, look! *Mars Attacks!* is a hit." But the studio didn't want to acknowledge that. It was a flop in America and that's the story they wanted to stick to. But it did well, and it's been making money ever since.

I was in pre-production on *The Treat** when the film was coming out. I remember having a meeting with an actress about doing one of the parts in *The Treat*. I got to the restaurant early and I'd just bought a copy of *Mad Magazine*, which had *Mars Attacks!* on the cover, and they'd done a Mort Drucker spoof of *Mars Attacks!* So, I bought it. And the spoof was really good, which wasn't easy to do because the movie is already like a *Mad Magazine* spoof.

I was looking through it, reading it, and this pretty girl comes up to my table, and she's a friend of the actress I'm going to interview, and she's come to tell me she's gonna be late. So, I thank her for telling me, and we sat there, me and this girl, waiting for the actress to arrive, and I said to her: "Oh, I'm just reading this *Mars Attacks!* thing in *Mad Magazine*."

And she said: "Oh, *Mars Attacks!* That's a terrible movie. Everybody says so."

---

* Starring Julie Delpy, Patrick Dempsey, Alfred Molina, Vincent Perez, and Michael York, directed by Jonathan Gems.

"Did you see it?" I asked her. I was interested to find out what she thought because everybody I knew loved the movie. But the reviews had been bad and, obviously, some people didn't like it, so I wanted to know why.

But she hadn't seen it. She'd heard it "from everyone" that it was no good. I thought, because she was about twenty-two years old, that if she saw it, she'd like it because most young people really loved it. But she hadn't seen it. She'd "heard" it was bad.

It was strange. There was a kind of anti-buzz about the film, but I was never able to meet anyone who'd seen it who didn't like it. And I did ask a lot of people. But I never got any criticism. Criticism is good. You want it. You want to know what people don't like. It's valuable. It helps you in your work. But I could never find anyone to tell me things they didn't like about the film. The whole release experience was very strange and unsatisfying.

MP: Well, them pulling it after two weeks, that determined that it couldn't be a hit in the United States. And my question is: Why they didn't want it to be a hit? Did you ever get an answer from anybody?

JG: No, never did. Nobody seemed to know. It was a mystery. I had this nice attorney named Melanie Cook. She was terrific. And she knew everything. The attorneys are the ones doing the legal stuff on all the deals being made, so they know everything that's going on.

I begged her to find out why we were getting these negative vibes, and she said she would. And, when she got back to me, she said she'd asked around but nobody knew anything. She acknowledged there was a negative buzz but no one knew why.

And Melanie Cook was well-connected. She heard everything. So, that was odd in itself.

MP: Okay. So, you wrote the treatment. What happened after that?

JG: Well, I revised it, the treatment, a few times, and when Tim was happy with it, he took a meeting at Warner Bros and pitched it to them. And they agreed to develop it, and called my agent to make a deal on the screenplay. It went very smoothly. No problem.

MP: No problem meaning?

JG: Well, you've got all these executives, quite a bureaucracy at Warner Bros, and they're connected to lots of people outside the studio – producers, agents, managers, attorneys. And they've all got an opinion. And they don't always commit to developing a film easily because everybody and his brother wants to have an opinion about it, and they wanna have meetings.

MP: How many meetings would they have, for example, before commissioning a film?

JG: That depends. One meeting, or half a dozen meetings. In this case, it was one. I didn't even go to it. Tim was protecting me. He went on his own. He came back and said: "We got it." And then I got a call from my agent saying to start work.

There was a deadline. Tim had to start pre-production by, I think it was March. So, I had to have the script ready by then.

This was in 1995, and the studio planned to start shooting in August and release the movie in August 1996.

This is what the studios do. They plan what films they're going to release and when they're gonna release them. And this is a complicated business because they have to talk to people at the other studios, so they don't release their big films at the same time. To some extent, the six major studios work together as a cartel. But they also compete. When it comes to distribution, they have to cooperate because if you've got *Star Wars* opening on August 4th, you don't wanna open your film on August 4th. So, you say like: "Can we release *Mars Attacks!* on August 18th then?" And you check around the other studios to see if that date's free.

And they'd done all that. Warner's had done all that. And, so they had a release date set up before they had the script.

Later on, they had to give up that date because we ran into a big problem with puppets. And because of those puppets, we lost almost six months.

MP: What was that problem with puppets?

JG: Well, Tim wanted to do the whole thing stop-motion. That's the old-fashioned way of doing 3-D animation. That's how he did *Nightmare Before Christmas*. Have you seen that?

MP: Yes, it's fantastic.

JG: Well, that's stop-motion. You have a figure, a puppet, and you move its foot a little bit, take a photograph. Then you move its foot a little bit more, take another photograph. Yeah, yeah, it's a very slow process. But it was a key component in Tim's vision for *Mars Attacks!* See, film is an art form and

Tim is a film buff, a film-enthusiast, and a film artist. He watches everything. His thirst for films is… unquenchable. It's a bit like painting, when you study all the other painters to see what they do, which helps you develop your own style. And Tim appreciated the artistry in movies like *Jason and the Argonauts* and *Earth vs the Flying Saucers*. He was a big fan of Ray Harryhausen who did the stop-motion for these films. And he wanted the Martians to be stop-motion.

I think he spoke to Henry Selick about it. He was the guy who did the stop-motion for *Nightmare Before Christmas*. And he's probably the best in the world at stop-motion. But he wasn't available. So, he went to the guys in England who did the stop-motion for *Wallace and Gromit*, who are pretty amazing.

So, one of the chief *Wallace and Gromit* guys, his name was Barry… Barry Purves. He came on to do the stop-motion. But he had to start from scratch, and set up a studio in L.A., and then recruit a big team, and that took a while. Then he started doing samples, and the samples were good. He was very good, Barry Purves, but Tim wanted the Martians to look a certain way, and make the movements the right sort of way, and it took a while to get there. And then, after a few months, they were up and running, and they were making these little figures, and then, two months later, they realized it was gonna take another four or five months. It was too long. It was too much time, and it was working out too expensive.

There was a great deal of despair at that moment. And Tim almost gave up doing the film. He was miserable and told me the movie was going to be canceled. We'd blown the schedule, you see, and the budget, and the release date, and there was a faction at the studio who wanted to shut us down.

And then, Larry Franco, our great, wonderful producer. Great, great guy. He fixed the problem. He flew up to see George Lucas in San Francisco. He's got that company Industrial Light & Magic. That was the most advanced special effects studio. Larry had just worked with them on *Jumanji*. D'you remember that?

MP: Yes. It was scary.

JG: Amazing special effects, weren't they?

MP: Yes.

JG: Well, at first, Tim was uncertain. He didn't really want to do it. He didn't think CGI was the way to go.

MP: What's CGI?

JG: Computer generated imagery. But this wasn't what Tim had in mind, and he was totally depressed, and getting ready to quit the movie. His whole vision of it was doing it stop-motion. But what Larry Franco did was, he asked Industrial Light & Magic if they could animate the Martians and make it look like stop-motion. Yeah, and it was a big challenge for them. But they like challenges. At that time, most of the animation they did was making things look real, not making them look fake. You know, they did all the *Star Wars* stuff.

And there was a bunch of guys at Industrial Light & Magic who said they could do it. And they wanted the gig. So, they got to work straightaway making a show-reel. And it was really good. It was rough. They did it very quickly. But you could see how a Martian, taken from Tim's drawings, looked in 3-D. And they did a short animation, and Tim was amazed. It really did look like stop-motion. So, the film was on again!

The only problem was the cost of it. It was a lot of money. And some people thought it was crazy because it was like using a modern, high-tech, robotic car factory to make a model T-Ford. Some of ILM's animation is cheap because they'd already developed the processes whereby they could animate rain, sea, clouds; they already had the program. But when you're inventing a new form of CGI, it means you have to develop new programming, new algorithms. You have to do it from scratch, which takes a lot of people working on it. So, it's expensive. And there was a lot of animation in the movie.

The whole credit sequence, with the Martian fleet taking off from Mars and traveling to earth was CGI. And then you had the Martians, and all their scenes, the spaceships, the robots, Sarah Jessica's head on the body of a chihuahua… The cost of the digital effects was huge. Around $37 million – that's what I heard.

MP: What about the puppet thing? Was that a big loss?

JG: I don't know how much it cost but yes, it was a big loss. That's when the studio started getting cold feet. It was a lot of money to waste. But yeah, so if you don't count the special effects, the movie cost roughly $33 million, which is very economical when you think of all the stars, and the locations, and the models, and the sets and costumes. It was very economical. It was only the CGI stop-motion that made it so expensive.

MP: But are you glad you did it stop-motion?

JG: Oh, for sure! It was brilliant. It was perfect. It was so clever because it made the Martians funny. And the things we had the Martians do were a series of jokes. This is the brilliance of Tim Burton. And it was great for Industrial Light & Magic because they were paid to develop all these useful new tools that they could use later on other movies.

MP: Hahaha! When I first watched *Mars Attacks!* I remember thinking I would have preferred to have modern special effects. That's what I personally didn't respond to. But now I think that's what's charming about it.

JG: Well, that was Tim's genius. Because everybody does that kind of slick animation. He wanted to do this, and it was essential for the nature of the comedy because it was so clunky.

MP: Yeah, clunky! Hahahaha! I wanted proper, super-powered spaceships and realistic Martians. But then it wouldn't have been so funny.

JG: Um, yeah. I'd forgotten all that trouble with the puppets. That was very stressful. Tim was going through all that while I was writing drafts. I did, I'm pretty sure, fourteen drafts of that script. It was brutal. 'Cause the studio kept telling me to hurry up. They'd give me a two-week deadline, or a three-week deadline. So, I'd write it in two weeks, deliver it; then they'd give me pages of notes, and bug me on the phone. Then they'd tell me to deliver the next draft in two weeks. So, I'd do another, and then another draft.

To be honest, I rarely followed any of their notes, which may be why they kept asking me for rewrites! But I didn't mind doing it, because every new draft made it better. I'd find more jokes, more twists, and more details. The more the studio's executives tried to change it, the more I'd refine it. Their attacks motivated me. It was like reverse encouragement. Luckily, I respond to abuse. I like criticism. It turns me on. They were weird, though, Warner Bros.

There was this group of executives at the studio who called themselves "The Creative Team." I never met them. I never had any meetings with them. I'd send in my draft, say the 4th draft; I'd send it over and, a few days later, I'd get back all these notes saying: "Oh change this, cut that scene, we don't like that character, delete paragraphs one, seven, and nine. You can't say this, you can't shoot dogs, you can't burn cows." All these instructions. What are you supposed to do?

I read the notes and if there was something good in there, I'd do it. But most of what they said, from my point of view, wasn't any good.

But I'd always be nice to them. I'd say: "Thank you very much for your notes. They're very helpful. Thank you for your input. It's much appreciated." And then I'd go ahead and write what I thought was best.

I learned this approach from watching actors in rehearsal when I was doing plays in London. The director would give an actor detailed notes about his performance, and the actor would say: "Oh, these are wonderful notes. Thank you so much." And then he'd ignore them! The nice approach is always best because, if you start arguing with them, you never hear the end of it, and things get personal, egos get involved, and before you know it, you're fighting a war. So, be nice. It's easier that way. And, for the most part, I got away with it.

MP: Maybe they didn't check to see that you followed their notes?

JG: That's quite possible. Sometimes they'd say: "Under no circumstances can you do that." And I'd think "Yeah, you can," and leave it in. And they'd never mention it again! Maybe they forgot? They're so busy all the time on different projects, different movies, and they're always having so many meetings, they don't know what day it is.

MP: And also, maybe they thought you were following their instructions?

JG: Yeah. And didn't bother to check. I was a bit naughty like that. They'd say: "Did you change it?" And I'd say: "Yeah." But I hadn't changed it. And I got away with it. Up until the problem with the cows. Did I tell you about that?

MP: Can you remind me, please?

JG: Sure. Well, it's important to have a good opening to your movie, right? And I had these cards, these great little oil paintings of Martian atrocities. And one of the cards showed a herd of stampeding cows, and they were on fire. So, I thought: "That's it! That's the opening. That's the opening of the film." You know, burning cows – the first sign that something is amiss.

So, you're in the Mid-West, in a prairie kind of farming area. It's peaceful. A farmhouse. Birds on a wire. Tractors. Two farmers meet up on the road, after a long day's work, and say howdy. And they smell something. Like: "What's that smell? Smells like hamburger. Somebody's having a barbecue." And then they hear a thundering noise. "What in the world is that?" And then, coming down the road, is a herd of stampeding cows and they're on fire!

A cold opening. No titles. A stampede of flaming cows. And it's really shocking. The family dog is crushed to death under their hooves. Then a flying saucer appears from behind the house and *bang!* Up comes the music, and the Warner Bros logo, and you start the title sequence.

I liked it. But the Creative Team said no, you can't have that because it's against the animal laws. You can't show animals being tortured or killed. There's a law against it. But my argument was: "It's not real. It's a visual effect. You're not really burning the cows. All you'd need is to get some cows to run down a road, or borrow some footage of a stampede, and superimpose the flames. You're not gonna hurt any cows."

You have to spell everything out in detail to them, which can be kind of exhausting. You also have to justify everything in the script on the level of why it's good, why the audience is going to like it. You not only have to write it, you have to sell every scene to them. It's grueling. But it's also not a bad thing. It makes you test everything, and it makes you work really hard.

But on some things, they were adamant. Adamant they had to go. After the first draft... After I delivered the first draft, there was a lot of things. For budget reasons. I wasn't thinking about the budget, I just let my mind run riot. And when they budgeted my script, it came out to, like, $170 million.

MP: Wow!

JG: Yeah. I wish they'd let us do that one! It would have been epic! I had scenes in New York City, some funny scenes in L.A. And scenes in Tokyo, Moscow, Beijing, London, Paris, Sydney, Australia, Cape Town, a paddy field in Vietnam, all kinds of places. That's my writing method, I overwrite.

You know about the two sides of the brain? The right-side, which is creative, and the left-side which is critical? Well, if you write with your critical mind, it's like driving with the handbrake on. It's torture. So, you switch it off. You write and you don't judge what you're doing. You just write whatever you want. That way, you get lots of stuff down on paper. Then, when it's finished, you go back over it, and clean it up.

Anyway, so, I had to cut out a lot of things for budget reasons, which was perfectly reasonable. I understood that. That was okay. And they told me what to cut, and I did a lot of that. But there were some things... Like, one scene I had with this cute little eight-year-old girl. She's got an ice-cream. I think this happened in New York, and the Martians are coming down Fifth Avenue, and she's kind of wide-eyed, and she offers them her ice-cream cone. She says: "Would you like some?" And they disintegrate her with their ray-guns.

They made me cut that out because it was cruelty to children. And the cows. They refused to allow the burning cows. They wouldn't budge on that.

MP: Well, this just shows me... I mean, in life, things like this happen.

JG: They do?

MP: I mean, maybe not Martians, but you know, tragedies. Tragedies happen. Children get killed. Cows do catch fire sometimes. Maybe there's lightning? Cows can burn. It can happen. It's not impossible. And yet you're not allowed to show that in a movie...

JG: Yeah. It's like political correctness, which is really just censorship – censoring speech, censoring ideas. And the rules are so random. You can have sex in a movie, that's okay, so long as you don't show any pubic hair. And you can kill as many people as you want but you can't kill children or animals. You can torture people and kill them in really nasty ways, like drive nails through their eyes, or chop them up with a machete, or put them through a wood-chipper. You can show a guy's head exploding, but you can't show a dog being killed. They made me cut a scene of a dog being killed. They said: "You can't show that." They forced me to cut it out.

MP: Didn't you have some birds being blown away? Wasn't there a dove, and some budgies?

JG: Well, yes. There was a dove, and the First Lady's budgies...

MP: But the dove is an animal!

JG: Well I know. They didn't say anything about that. It made no sense! But making me cut out the dog was absurd. But I think it was just because the V.P. (Vice President) in charge of development, I think his title was – he started getting a bit egotistical. He wasn't getting enough attention. He wanted to put his thumb on the print, as it were. And he told me to get rid of the family dog being killed by the stampeding cows, and he was very insistent about it. So, I had to do it. It was an ego thing. He was demonstrating his authority.

But there was another scene where the Martian Girl, she goes into the president's bedroom to assassinate the president, and she misses and kills the president's dog. So, you *do* have a dog being killed, and they didn't say anything about that. Go figure!

MP: You know what comes to mind? There were so many things being killed by the Martians that they gave up in the end! Hahaha!

JG: Yeah! We had battles over every draft on that front, but mostly they let me have my way because I fought so hard. But with the cows, they dug their heels in. They consistently said: "You can't have that opening. That's not… We won't do that. That's against the rules. We absolutely will not shoot that, so cut it out. If you wanna have a pre-credit sequence, think of something else. But we're not having the burning cows. No way. That's not happening."

So, I tried. I tried to accommodate them. I tried to be flexible. But every time, on every new draft, I would leave dealing with the cows 'til last. I would rewrite the whole thing, then go back to the beginning and look at the cows. I was hoping I'd think of something else – something better.

I asked Tim about it and he said he liked the burning cows, but if I came up with something better, that would be okay too. But I could *never* think of anything better. So, when it came to the deadline, I would submit the script, and it would still have the cows.

Finally, they told me: "If those cows are in the next draft, you're fired." They were really serious about it. But I didn't know whether to believe them. And, on the next draft, I still thought the cows were the best idea, so they were still in it. And that's when I got fired.

MP: Oh, my God! So, what happened? Did you get rehired?

JG: Eventually. But I was fired. I was off the picture. The studio told Tim he couldn't have me anymore.

MP: Wow. That must have felt terrible.

JG: Well, it did and it didn't. I was pretty burnt out by that point. I'd done about twelve drafts under all this pressure and I was knackered. It was actually a relief to be fired. And I recommended Scott Alexander and Larry Karazewski to take over. I figured they'd do a good job. I had a lot of respect for Scott and Larry. And I trusted Tim. So, I thought it would be okay. The movie was what was important, not my ego. And it meant I could have a rest.

So, Scott and Larry worked on it for about five weeks. I think they were given three weeks to fix the script but their first draft wasn't... There were problems with it, so they did a second draft.

MP: What did you do during the rest?

JG: Well, after having a break, I started work on *The Treat*. An independent company called Cineville run by a guy called Carl Colpaert was interested in it. A friend of mine, named Emma Makinen, had spoken to him about it. So, I started work on the screenplay, which was based on a play I wrote with my mother, Pam.* It was a nice change of pace. And a change is as good as a rest.

---

* Pam Gems, playwright.

MP: So, what happened next?

JG: Well, I was working on *The Treat*, and not thinking about *Mars Attacks!* And about three weeks later, I got a call from Tim. He was kind of down. He said Scott and Larry had done a draft, but there was something wrong with it, so they were doing another one. And he asked what I was doing. So, I told him, and I didn't hear from him again until about two weeks later, when he called me and asked me to go up and see him in Ojai.

Now, Ojai is this beautiful little town north of L.A., near Ventura. And it's in a valley. You've got the mountains on either side of you, and it's a North-South valley, which is rare. Most of the valleys in the world go East-West. And when you get a valley that goes North-South, it feels different. It has a magical feel to it. They say the feng-shui is special, and it certainly feels like that.

I went there to Ojai originally because of a big apartment building at the bottom of my hill in Hollywood. This rather fetching, 1930's high-rise apartment building was called The Ojai. In the States, they give names to buildings, which is really cool. And this one was called The Ojai. And I used to look at it every time I walked down the hill to Hollywood Boulevard. Someone told me Joan Crawford lived there before she was famous. But I never knew how to say that word 'Ojai.' Was it like O-Jay? Like orange juice?

So, one day, as I was passing, I saw a guy come out of the building, so I stopped him and asked him how to pronounce the name. "How do you say it?" And he said: "It's pronounced 'O-hi.'" Isn't that nice? It's like: "Oh, hi, how are you doing?"

And then, later on, I was looking at a map, and I saw this place, Ojai, on the map. So, I thought: I'm gonna go there.

I'm gonna check it out. And then I met this girl at a party whose name was Aura. Hippy parents, right? So, I asked her if she was raised on a commune. And she said, yes, in Ojai. So, I thought: "That's a sign. I must go there."

So, one weekend, I drove up there and discovered this little town, full of bookstores with rare second-hand books, and shops selling organic vegetables with the dirt still on them, and I fell in love with it. It was like an old western town, with wooden sidewalks, inhabited by self-sufficiency types, ex-hippies, home-schoolers and freethinkers. And I found out that one of my heroes, Krishnamurti, had lived there. And you could visit his place, which they'd made into a kind of museum. A shrine to Krishnamurti. So, I walked around it – this nice, Nepalese style house with libraries and gardens. It had an amazingly peaceful atmosphere.

And, when I got home, after about a two-hour drive, I told Tim about it. I said it would be a perfect place to write, away from the storm and strife of L.A. And I told him I was gonna buy a place there. A cheap apartment, or a shack or something, and write my scripts there. So, I was planning to do that.

And a couple of weeks later – it was a weekend, Saturday – I told Tim I was going up to Ojai to visit real estate agents and look for somewhere to buy. At that time, I had about $30,000 in the bank. And he said: "Why don't we come with you?"

So, he and Lisa-Marie came with me.

MP: Oh, he's so sweet! He probably thought, because he had more money than you, he could buy a house for himself and let you write there.

JG: Well, I don't know about that. But what happened was we had this lovely drive up there, stopping off at places. Tim liked all those Americana things, like *Frostee Freeze*. I remember we stopped at *Frostee Freeze* and sat on benches, like picnic tables, and had frosties and corn dogs. And, I think we stopped at an *In-N-Out Burger*. I remember saying to Tim: "You know why they call it 'In and Out Burger'?" He said "No." And I said: "It's because it goes in here (pointing to mouth) and comes out of here." (Pointing to rear end).

MP: Haha!

JG: And when we got to Ojai, Lisa-Marie really perked up. She liked it instantly. She's a very spiritual person, very sensitive spiritually. And she got excited. I remember her pointing out a slim, very erect, straight-backed lady with masses of white hair, in a beautiful blue-green sari walking down the sidewalk. And later on, she actually met this lady who, it turned out was 103 years old, and had been the girlfriend of Marcel Duchamp.

Anyway, we went into the office of this real estate agent, and I was looking at pictures of what they had. And there was almost nothing in my budget range. And Tim and Lisa were looking around, and Tim saw a black and white photograph of an old Spanish-style house. When he drew my attention to it, I thought it was there for decoration. It looked like a tintype from the Old West – the kind of place where the mayor used to live in, say, 1900. But Tim asked the real estate lady about it, and she said: "Well, it's for sale."

It turned out they'd had the place on their books for thirteen years and couldn't sell it. It was unsaleable. But Tim said: "Can we go see it?" And she said: "Well, we can. We've got the keys. But it's in very bad condition. I don't know if it's gonna be worth your time."

But Tim wanted to see it, so we followed the real estate agent in the car, and we drove out of town, and up this hill, which was kind of forested. Lots of oak trees. And, finally, we got to this gate. And when I saw the gate, I thought: "Oh-oh." It looked like the gate in...

MP: (Interrupting) *Edward Scissorhands*!

JG: Yes! How did you know?

MP: I was gonna say.

JG: Yeah, that's what it looked like. And I remember getting out, and the ground was covered in acorns. And the real estate lady was trying to open the gate, and me and Tim gave her a hand, and we pulled it open, and it squeaked – iiiiiii! Like out of a horror movie. And then we go up this drive and there are these big oak trees on either side, making a canopy over the drive, so it's dark. It's like going through a tunnel, with the sun flickering through the leaves.

So, we go up this drive. Oh, my God. Then we go up to the top – to the top of the hill – and we come out of the trees and there's this incredible house! It looked like something out of the 1920's, but old Spanish style. It was all, well most of it, on one storey. There was a smaller part where there was a second storey. And it looked like, I don't know, PickFair, or something. You know, where Mary Pickford and Douglas Fairbanks lived. It was redolent of the 1920's. The Silent Era. The Jazz Age. Scott Fitzgerald. Flappers. All that.

Then we go up to the front door. This big door. And it's like a heavy oak door, and when the lady opened it, it creaked – a long, drawn-out creak. Tim had gone very quiet. I could tell he was excited. But then there was a horrible smell. It was the worst smell you could imagine. Awful. It was so bad, it almost made you want to throw up.

Tim said: "What's that smell? It's pretty bad."

The real estate agent said: "Yes, yes, you see, the two old ladies who used to live here, they had a lot of cats. And they let them pee wherever they wanted. And all the floorboards got soaked with cat piss." She said it was impossible to get rid of it. The smell was just soaked into the fabric of the house.

MP: Hahaha! That's why nobody bought it, for thirteen years! Yuck!

JG: Yeah, but Tim was enchanted with it. He loved it. You had the front of the house which was kind of grand, like a Spanish-American hacienda. Later on, Tim called it "the haunted hacienda." And then, you go around the back and there was a kidney-shaped swimming pool, which was derelict, but it was nice. And there was a wonderful view. 'Cause we were on top of a hill, facing west. You could see for miles. Forest and then some fields and more forest, and hills, and mountains in the distance. On the north side of the property there was a golf course, but it was very quiet. It was the edge of the golf course, and we never saw anyone there. You really felt like you were on your own, surrounded by Nature. Beautiful. So, I knew straight away Tim wanted to buy it. And he did. He did buy it.

MP: Wow!

JG: He spent a lot of money on it. It took many months. They took out the floorboards. All the floorboards in the house, including the joists. And they put in new floors. It was the only way to get rid of the smell. They did a lot of work on the roof. Re-tiling it. Um, and then the rooms. Bit by bit, each room was renovated. Some of the walls were re-plastered. It was a helluva job, with new copper pipes, new plumbing, and the whole place was rewired.

The rooms were lovely, well-proportioned with high ceilings, apart from the basement, which Tim turned into a movie theater. The architecture was good. That was the point. It was very well designed. And Tim was very nice. He dedicated one of the rooms to me. He said: "Look. This is your room." He was holding out a key. "Whenever you wanna get out of L.A. to have a break, or write something, you can come here."

MP: I had a feeling. When you wanted to go and buy a property, and he said he wanted to go with you, I thought he knows he's got more money than Jonny, and he wants to fulfill your wish.

JG: Do you think?

MP: Well, he knew you wanted to go there, and rest and write, and he happened to see this amazing place. So, in a way, he did it for both of you. He wanted the place and he did you a favor because now you wouldn't have to spend $30,000. That was really lovely. I want to be like this.

JG: Well, he's a generous guy, that's true. So, he was there, up in Ojai, and he called me and said: "Can you come up here and read the latest draft of *Mars Attacks!?*" So, of course I went.

I drove up there. And I arrived, and we were in the kitchen, and he gave me the script. I remember it was a hot day, and he had food and orange juice all ready. He said: "Here it is.

Here's the latest version. It's got notes. Have a read, and see what you think."

So, I said: "What do *you* think of it?"

And he said: "Well, you know, there's some problems, but I don't wanna tell you what I think. Just go ahead and read it."

So, after a snack, I went out by the pool, and sat under a big cedar tree, in the shade of this big, beautiful tree, and I was drinking orange juice and reading the script. And it wasn't too bad. It wasn't much different. There were cuts. The burning cows had gone, of course. And other things the Creative Team wanted cut because they were too gross or too weird. But some of the dialogue was better. Scott and Larry had put in some witty lines. But it flowed and the story, characters, scenes, and structure were the same. So, I was thinking: "Well, this isn't too bad. What's the problem?"

See, I'd picked up a vibe from Tim that something disastrous had happened to the script. But he was being non-committal. He didn't want to influence me. So, maybe the script was okay, and he just wanted me to confirm that? So, I was reading it slowly and carefully, because I wanted to give Tim an honest and well-considered assessment. And I was about halfway through when Lisa-Marie came down the steps, looking dazzlingly beautiful in the sunshine, and said: "It's lunch time!"

She'd made some lunch up at the house. Okay, great. So, we walked back up together. It was a super-hot, sunny day. It must have been July or August. And I always liked walking with Lisa because she has a gossamer-light atmosphere and always smelled so nice. She's a Sagittarius and I like Sagittarians because my Venus is in Sagittarius. But I think she has some Gemini in her chart too because she's very light. I wouldn't have been surprised if she'd levitated. Although, when she's angry, the Sagittarian comes out. She explodes like a fire-bomb. And it can be scary! But that didn't happen often. Hardly ever.

Anyway, we were in the kitchen, having lunch – something Lisa-Marie had made that was healthy and salady and organic – and Tim said: "So, how's the script?"

I said: "Pretty good. I don't see any major problems."

He said: "How far have you got?"

"About halfway."

He said: "Wait 'til you read the rest of it."

So, after lunch, I went back down the steps, past the pool, to the round concrete table under the cedar tree, and read the rest of the script. And it was terrible. Shockingly terrible.

Scott and Larry had changed the whole last act of the movie. Oddly, enough – and this was a truly bizarre coincidence – it was very similar to the third act of *Independence Day*, where the world is saved by the military and the president.

Their rewrite had abandoned the theme, the raison d'être of the movie, and turned the last act into a series of comic-book action sequences where heroic characters defeat the Martians. You know, the first two acts built up the characters and the situations so they can pay off in the third act. But, in this draft, nothing paid off. It was just a predictable, cliché climax, and all the satire was lost.

It was actually the kind of thing the Creative Team probably liked because they could understand it. It was what they were used to. So, it's possible Scott and Larry were doing what the studio wanted. I don't know. But it didn't work. It fell flat. And it wasn't funny. So, I was... well, I was kind of shaken by it. It was like that feeling you get when you go home, open the door, and see your flat has been burgled.

So, I went back up the steps, and found Tim in his art studio.

He said: "Have you finished it?"

I said: "Yes."

He said: "What do you think?"

I said: "It's a mess."

And he said: "Let's go in the living room."

So, we went into the living room and sat down. I sat on the sofa. He sat on the armchair. He liked to sit with his legs dangling over the armrest. And he looked at me and said: "So, can you fix it?"

At that point, my mind was a complete blank. I didn't know if I could fix it or not. I was a little bit in shock. You know how, when you're in shock, you don't feel any pain? Well, I didn't feel any pain at all. I was in limbo. And I couldn't think. So, I just let my mouth do the talking. Tim wanted me to fix it, so I said: "Yeah."

But I didn't know how to do it. I was kind of shaken.

But Tim was very calm. He can sometimes flip out over small things but, when it's something big, he gets very relaxed and calm. Very focused. He's good in a crisis. "How long is it gonna take you?" And I said: "Three weeks." This was a wild guess, but usually three weeks is long enough to do most things.

And then he said: "Can you do it in a week?"

Well, this was another shock. A *week?* Was he serious? There was no way I could redo the script in a week. It needed a lot of work. It wasn't possible. I hated to say no to him but I had to. "No, I can't do it in a week," I said. "It's not possible."

"Well, that's gonna be tough," he said. For some reason, the script had to be fixed in a week.

"You can get started right away. Stay here and do it, and me and Lisa-Marie will look after you. I'm gonna be drawing and painting pictures for the movie. You can talk to me anytime you want, if you have any problems with it, or you wanna discuss anything."

I couldn't believe he expected me to come up with a new script in a week. See, I knew I couldn't go back to my previous draft because the studio wouldn't buy it. The rewrite would have to look different. "But I don't think I can do it in a week," I said.

"I think you can," said Tim. "I have faith in you."

Well, that did it. When he said that, I couldn't say no, could I? So, I said "okay." But I didn't feel good about it. I felt kind of doomed. Then he took me round the house to find a writing room. I chose a small room, which wasn't really a room, it was an alcove, next door to his painting studio.

It would give me a sense of reassurance, knowing he was next door. Whenever I got stuck, I could go next door and talk to him about it.

I was in a panic because I really didn't think I could do it. You see, it was a hard job. Not only did I have to completely rewrite the second half, and revise the first half, but I had to do it so the studio would accept it. I couldn't go back to my previous draft. I had to make it look new. And I had to type it out, all 120 pages, nice and neat and professional, or the studio wouldn't respect it. I couldn't cut and paste things. This was before we had word processors.

I asked him: "Why does it have to be so quick? Maybe, if I busted a gut, I could do it in *two* weeks."

But he said it's gotta be one week because there was gonna be a meeting at Warner Bros in one week to decide whether or not to drop the project.

Well, the studio had threatened to cancel *Mars Attacks!* before and hadn't done it, right? But this time was different. I'd been away from the fray for a month and, coming back, it was like I was returning to the trenches and seeing more casualties, more blast holes, more dead horses, and a big loss in morale. It felt like the war was being lost. And, despite his composure, Tim had an air of weariness, of fatigue.

You have to be resilient to be a movie director in Hollywood 'cause they really put you through the wringer. Look what they did to Orson Welles, Preston Sturges, Charlie Chaplin, all of them. And I could see why, this time, Warner's might really close it down. They'd wasted a lot of money on the puppets, we'd missed the release date, they'd had problems with me on the script, and now with Scott and Larry as well, and this was holding everything up, with a whole lot of people on salary who couldn't do anything because, without the script, they couldn't budget, or schedule, or book soundstages or start building anything. Nothing could happen, and it was costing Warner's a fortune. And there was all this studio politics going on as well, so it was a real emergency. I had to do the script in a week.

So, I kind of plotted out my work schedule. I had seven days. How much could I do in a day? Well, I could do *this much*. Then I calculated how many days I'd need based on *this much*, and it turned out to be fifteen days.

So, I had to find a way to cut corners. How could I do fifteen days' work in seven days? The only way I could do it was to go back to my last draft, and rewrite it using different words, add some of Scott and Larry's bits, lay it out differently on the page, and present it as a fresh new script. And to get it done in seven days, I needed to type 17 or 18 pages a day. This was a tall order.

Tim could see I was having an anxiety attack, and it seemed to amuse him. This helped me actually. It's this thing he has: everything's a game. Why freak out? It's only a movie. And he casually suggested we put up an 8-by-4 soft-board on the wall, and write the scenes and the character's names on pieces of paper, and pin them to the board.

So, we did this, and it gave me an overview – and the rewrite began to seem less daunting. It gave me an illusion of control. And it helped his process too, I think, because, as time went on, he filled the board with more and more drawings, and his vision of the film became more defined. He visualized each scene by drawing its chief elements and this, in turn, helped me with the writing.

And when I hit a road-block, I went next door, and we talked about it, and played with Tim's pictures on the board, and came up with solutions.

So, I started work by rewriting my last draft, and improving it, thanks to Tim's soft-board. I worked fast, like I was on speed, banging out the script on my electric typewriter fueled by adrenaline.

And Lisa-Marie, now and again, would come into my alcove, like an angel from heaven, with a cup of tea or a glass of cucumber juice. She was my muse. She was Tim's muse as well. She was so lovely, you just wanted to please her.

I'd written the Martian Girl for her, and later on, I thought she'd like Poppy to be in the movie as well. And, when I told her I was writing Poppy into the script, she was thrilled.

MP: Why did you put her chihuahua in the film?

JG: I thought Lisa-Marie would like it. They were inseparable. They really were. She took Poppy with her everywhere. So,

Poppy became part of the story, as the pet of Sarah Jessica Parker's character, which was a little bit based on Lisa-Marie. And then I discussed it with Tim. He was uncertain at first because Poppy hadn't been trained. She wasn't a performing dog, so it wasn't practical. She might cause trouble on the set. But, after being dubious, he came up with this crazy idea...

Okay, let me back-track a little. I'd written a scene where the Martians do medical experiments on Donald Kessler, the scientist, played by Pierce Brosnan, and the TV presenter played by Sarah Jessica Parker. And then Tim came up with the idea of the Martian surgeons grafting Sarah Jessica's head on to Poppy's body. After that, he was devoted to having Poppy in the movie and he started drawing lots of cute pictures of her.

MP: I love that scene. Some people think it's really sad though.

JG: Yeah, well it *is* sad. But it's also completely ridiculous! Actually, when Tim first suggested it, I couldn't see how it could work. I mean, how can you put a human head on a chihuahua's body? But Tim just said: "It's easy!" So, I trusted he knew what he was doing. But I was very curious to see how that was going to turn out!

MP: It was great. I loved that bit.

JG: Yeah, the "star-crossed lovers." Ha ha. So, there I was in Ojai, writing the new script as fast as I could, and Lisa-Marie was looking after me, and Tim. And so was Poppy. She was such an affectionate little dog. Full of love. Poppy would come in, jump on my lap and curl up there while I was typing. And Lisa would come in looking for her and lean over my shoulder to read what I was doing. Then she'd ask questions and make suggestions. She had this wonderful life-force. It kind of buoyed me up.

I said before that she was light – light in the same way Sarah Jessica is light in the movie – but she's also strong. She was like a strong breeze that keeps you flying.

And she took care of both of us. She cleaned the kitchen, and went shopping for supplies, and made fun meals that were sometimes healthy vegan-type dishes, with all kinds of exotic vegetables, and sometimes hamburgers and thick-cut fries, or pancakes with maple syrup – and she had a blender she used to make delicious smoothies. And she filled the house with aromatic candles. They were everywhere, in the hallways, the stairs, the kitchen, everywhere. Lisa-Marie liked everything to smell nice. And she always smelled nice herself, like apple blossom.

And, when Tim first bought the house, she'd planted sunflowers out front. And these sunflowers all came out. They hit their peak while I was doing the rewrite. It was like a miracle, those sunflowers. And they're spooky, sunflowers. They move their faces with the sun. So, in the morning, you'd see hundreds of sunflowers facing east and, at the end of the day, their heads were facing west.

It was inspiring being there with Tim. He was in the art studio next door, working away, and he's a terrific artist. He was doing these great pictures, and trying out different designs for the Martian Girl's costume, and drawing and painting the Martians – trying out different styles for their uniforms. And so, when I had my coffee break, I'd go into his studio and look at what he'd done. And it gave me energy.

And he was very comfortable to hang out with, and we would kind of joke around. And he would give me ideas. So, the writing conditions were great.

There's nothing better than being around other artists. They understand and support what you're doing. They give you permission to go for broke. You can see why some people like to form artists' colonies. I've never been in one, or known many artists. My mother was an artist. We had a colony of two. Me and Tim, we were a colony of two as well. Well, three, with Lisa. Oh, I've just remembered something! Lisa-Marie was teaching Poppy to talk! She was teaching her dog to talk. It was so funny. I think she was angling for Poppy to have a speaking part. Hahaha! And you could see Poppy working hard on it. She loved Lisa so much she really wanted to please her. And one day, I think it was in the art studio, Lisa-Marie came in with Poppy, holding the dog in her arm, and she looked at her, in a fierce kind of way, and went: "Poppy! Poppy!"

And Poppy went: "I la-yow!"

Tim said: "What? What's she saying?"

"Do it again, Poppy," said Lisa. "Poppy! Poppy!"

And Poppy went: "I la yow."

"I love you," said Lisa. "She's saying 'I love you.'"

And Poppy went: "I la yow!"

We were so impressed. She got the dog to talk!

But Lisa-Marie wasn't sweetness and light all the time. She got frustrated sometimes because me and Tim were working and ignoring her. When I was hard at work, I didn't want to be disturbed and so she would go talk to Tim, and he didn't want to be disturbed either. So, she got frustrated.

One day, she came into my alcove and I didn't want to talk to her. So, she did this incredible flying kick. She was very athletic, and she aimed the kick at my head. I ducked just in time, and her foot went "whack!" into the wall behind me. Really hard. It was like a karate kick and she was wearing boots. She could have knocked me out!

But she was the most beautiful girl you've ever seen; so beautiful it made you feel good to look at her. And she's very sweet-natured usually.

MP: That must have inspired you, having a beautiful girl there while you're writing. If she wasn't there, it would have been very different – just you and Tim.

JG: You're right. She was an inspiration. Lisa-Marie was Tim's muse – and mine as well. She was like the goddess Athena, and we were doing it all for her. She was exquisite. A wild and wonderful girl.

So, I was in my alcove, writing the script as fast as I could, and really worried because of the time. I had so little time to get the script done. I was working around the clock, and sleeping about three hours a night. But, after three days, I could see I was gonna make it. I was gonna get it done in a week. And I remember being at breakfast with Tim, feeling a little less stressed, and saying: "I think I'm gonna make it. I'll have it done in four days."

And he said: "No, no. It's gotta be done by Friday."

That was in two days! So, I said: "No, Monday. It's Monday. I'll get it done by Monday. You said I had a week."

And he said: "Yeah. But a week is five days."

MP: Hahahaha! Oh God!

JG: Hahaha! I thought he meant seven days. But the Warner's meeting was Friday afternoon! And so, that was really hard. I didn't sleep at all for the next two nights and worked like fuck, drinking lots of black coffee and, somehow, I did it. I finished typing the script Friday morning, just before they had to leave to go to L.A. It was another one of those god-awful cliff-hangers.

So, Tim and Lisa went down to L.A., and I went to bed. And when they got back I was still sleeping.

MP: What happened at the meeting?

JG: Nothing. The executives were going to read it over the weekend, and let us know their decision on Monday.

MP: Oh, my God.

JG: But Tim said they'd issued notices to everyone on the payroll. A week's notice. 'Cause you have to do that – give them a week's notice, before you fire them. So, they'd done that. And they'd given Tim a week's notice at the meeting. They weren't kidding about canceling the film.

I slept most of the weekend and then, on Monday, Tim got a call. The head honchos had read the script and, after much discussion, they had decided not to cancel. The film would go ahead.

MP: Oh, thank God!

JG: Yeah, it was a huge relief. It would have been tragic if they'd canceled it. I think, for Tim, *Mars Attacks!* was the hardest movie to get made up to that point. Later on, he had a harder one – *Superman Lives*, with Nicolas Cage – which they *did* cancel.

MP: Nicolas Cage was going to play Superman?

JG: Yeah. I would've loved to have seen that.

MP: Yeah!

JG: Well, it was a great relief. And I was pleased for myself, and for Tim, and for Lisa-Marie. I thought she had star quality. I'd urged Tim to give her the role of Vampira in *Ed Wood*, which he did, and she was good in that but, unfortunately, he had to re-voice her. This was a blow. And I think she felt like she'd failed. But she hadn't had any voice-training. Most actors need to train their voices. Lisa hadn't done that. After Vampira, she started taking voice lessons.

MP: To be honest, I really liked that – that great big voice of Vampira's. It works really well in the movie.

JG: Yeah, I know. But that's not Lisa-Marie, which was a serious disappointment for her, and bad for her self-esteem. And it was a double problem because not only did she think she'd failed professionally, but she'd also failed her boyfriend who she really wanted to impress. So, the Martian Girl was important to her. It was her chance to prove herself. And she worked very hard on it. And she was great in it.

MP: She was! For a lot of people, she's the best character in the movie!

JG: I actually wrote a short film to showcase her acting. It was called *Somewhere to Park My Bike*. I wrote the script, got the locations, got the cast – Glenn Shadix was gonna be in it – and I found a good cameraman, and an editor, and some crew people, and then, I can't remember. There was a problem with time. I didn't have the time to do it. Lisa-Marie said yes to it. It was a nice part for her. She was the lead. And it would've shown off her acting. And it's one of my regrets that we never made that film. It was only gonna be about twelve minutes long, but it would have been nice. I wish we'd done it.

MP: I was surprised she wasn't in *The Treat*.

JG: That's true. Well, I did ask her. She was the first person I asked. And she turned me down! Why, I don't know. She would have been amazing in it. I couldn't understand her reaction. She didn't like the script. She said it should be more like Russ Meyer. But Russ Meyer made soft-porn movies and *The Treat* wasn't a soft-porn movie. It's a character-driven comedy about men's fantasies about women.

But I didn't give up on her. I wrote another film for her called *The Beatnicks*. A friend of mine, Kevin Williams, who lived near me on Whitley Heights, had written and directed a black and white short film called *The Beatnicks*. I suggested expanding it into a full-length movie. I said I'd write and produce it, and he could star and direct.

Kevin Williams was happy with this, so I wrote the screenplay, expanded the story, and created a role for Lisa-Marie. Her character's name was Nicolette, I remember. She was the love interest. I worked out a budget and a schedule. It was gonna be a three-week shoot and cost around $300,000.

At one point, Tim was interested in coming in as executive producer, which basically means finding the money. But he had a meeting with Kevin Williams, who was going to direct, and I don't think that went well, and he pulled out. He may have been right because, after that, there were all kinds of problems with the project and I bailed out too.

A very altered version of *The Beatnicks* was made much later. I didn't have anything to do with it. Lisa-Marie played a small part in it, although it wasn't the part I'd written for her.

MP: I don't know this movie.

JG: Yeah, it's still called *The Beatnicks*. I've got it somewhere.

MP: Has it been released? How come I never heard of it? How long is it?

JG: Ninety minutes.

MP: Really?

JG: Yes. And she's in it.

MP: Gosh, I never knew this. I wanna see it. Do you have the script?

JG: I think so. Somewhere.

MP: Can I read it?

JG: Yeah, if I can find it. The film I wrote was quite charming, like Kevin Williams's short. Romantic, and done in that beatnik style, all hip and flip. Everybody's being cool, but they're living an illusion. It was a soufflé, very light, whimsical and kind of melancholy. You should see the short film. Kevin's short film. It's good.

INTERVIEW 2

MP: So, I wanted to ask you about plagiarism. I've heard a lot of that goes on in Hollywood. Is that true?

JG: Sure, it goes on all the time. It's inevitable, when you think about it, because you have all these people who want to make movies, and to do that they need an idea, a story, a script. And a good idea that you can sell to a studio is not easy to find. So, people are stealing ideas all the time. It's a free-for-all. And, as for copyright, well, forget it. Unless you have buckets of money to pay lawyers.

There are a small handful of cases – personally, I only know of two – where a story was stolen and the author went to court and won compensation. Art Buchwald. Art Buchwald did it. He sued Paramount for stealing a story and he won. But Art Buchwald was married to an immensely rich woman who was prepared to spend millions on the case, so the studio settled. The other case was *Terminator* and *The Matrix*, which were both conceived and written by Sophia Stewart who wasn't credited or paid for them. She spent years and years fighting in the courts and, eventually, after years of torture and struggle, she got a judgment in her favor.

But these are exceptional cases. Very exceptional. Here's the problem: there's no point in suing a studio if they make a film out of your story, because they're protected by armies of lawyers and their pockets are way, way deeper than yours. So, if you take them to court you will lose, and end up having to sell your house to pay the lawyers' fees.

The other thing is studios, as a rule, don't sue other studios. And you can see why. If they started suing one another for stolen stories, it would never end. So, if you write a story and you sell it to, say, Sony, and someone else gets to hear of it, and sells the same story to Disney – and Disney gets their film into production before Sony – well, Sony could sue, right? But they don't. Most times, they will simply shrug their shoulders and, if it's not too late, drop the project.

No studio wants to plan the release of a movie about, say, Abraham Lincoln, if another studio is releasing a movie about Abraham Lincoln. So, that's how it goes. And that's why people aren't afraid to steal ideas and stories. There's no way to effectively enforce copyright.

I witnessed it a lot. I remember an Italian guy, a writer and art director, who'd come to L.A. with his screenplay. He'd taken it to various producers, pitching it, and it was stolen. And they made the film. And the poor guy was crying on my shoulder about it. But there was nothing he could do. He was on a visitor's visa and he had to go back to Italy.

But plagiarism isn't only rampant in Hollywood, it's throughout the entire movie industry. I remember one screenwriter I knew who wrote an original screenplay – all his own idea – and he sold it to a French film company. He was paid for it, so that was good. And the film was made, so that was good too. And it was successful, so that was even better. But he didn't get a credit. No credit. Because the producers used the name of a French screenwriter because that would help them. My friend's name didn't mean anything in France, but the name they put on the screen as the writer, was known in France, and it helped the film get accepted by the Cannes Film Festival, and helped it get good reviews from the French critics.

These things happen. I had ideas, stories and scripts stolen quite a few times. And there was nothing I could do about it. I spoke to people about it but they all said: "Don't worry about it. It happens to everybody." And it does.

Here's an example. One night, in my little Hollywood house, I watched the movie *Sabrina* on TV. It's by Billy Wilder, who did *The Apartment* and *Some Like It Hot*, and all these other great films. And I watched it, and it was good. Witty, romantic, great roles for actors. And then it fell to pieces. It belly-flopped. It had the wrong ending.

Basically, in the story, Audrey Hepburn is wooed by two brothers. The young, sexy one who is penniless, fun-loving and irresponsible, and the older brother, played by Humphrey Bogart, who is boring and conservative but is a very successful businessman.

Audrey marries Bogart. Wrong! Wrong! Wrong! It leaves a bad taste in your mouth because it's not romantic. She should have married the younger brother. Who cares about money? Love is more important than money. Big mistake on Billy Wilder's part. And when *Sabrina* came out – even with its big stars, William Holden, Audrey Hepburn and Humphrey Bogart – it was a box office bomb. People didn't like it.

So, anyway, the next day, after seeing *Sabrina* on TV, I had a meeting at Paramount. They wanted me to write a script for them, but I didn't like the subject matter. So, I was in this executive's office, talking about it, and she had to go out for a few moments, so I started snooping around her office. And I saw, on top of her TV, a new VHS tape of *Sabrina*. So, when the executive came back, I talked about *Sabrina* and how it had bombed but if it was remade with a different ending, it would be a hit. And she said – the development executive – "Okay, why don't you write it?"

So, a deal was made, and I spent the next three months writing *Ramona*. The same basic story as *Sabrina* but, this time, the Audrey Hepburn character is a beautiful Mexican girl, and she ends up with the sexy, younger brother.

Well, I delivered the script. This was the first draft. And they loved it. I was taken to meet the president of Paramount, and he shook my hand, and said: "We're making it." The D-girl was very happy about it. It was a big feather in her cap.

MP: The what? The what girl?

JG: D-Girl. That's what they call development executives. She was happy, and we had a meeting with some executives about who should produce it. This was all happening, I'm not sure, around 1992. And we talked about directors. And that was funny because they all came up with different names and then I said: "How about Billy Wilder? Why not get Billy Wilder to direct it?" And they all said: "No. He's dead."

MP: What?

JG: But he wasn't dead. He was fine. He was old, but he was fine. He was in good health.

MP: Oh, my God!

JG: Anyway, I didn't want to contradict them. I told Tim about it later and we had a laugh about it. But then disaster struck.

The head of Paramount was replaced by a new guy who canceled all the previous president's projects. So, that was the end of that. Except, a year later, I read in *Variety*, Paramount was going to remake *Sabrina*. And they did it. They did it with Scott Rudin producing and Harrison Ford in the Bogart role. They did a straight copy of the original. And maybe to distance themselves from *Ramona*, they didn't change the ending. And so, just like the original, it bombed.

MP: Oh, Jesus.

JG: You know, Woody Allen is famous for never sending his scripts out – even to his own agent. Because, when he started, he would send his script to people – agents, producers, actors – and all the jokes would get stolen. They'd show up on TV a month later, so he couldn't use them anymore. So, he learned to hide his scripts. And it's the same with everybody. It happened with *Mars Attacks!* We tried to keep it secret but the Topps Company, which owned the cards, let the cat out of the bag. They publicized that Tim Burton and Warner Bros were going to make *Mars Attacks!* This was a disaster, and almost put an end to the project.

The trouble was that the title *Mars Attacks!* tells you what the movie's about. And what happened was all the other studios started talking about doing sci-fi movies. See, people rushed to copy what Tim Burton was doing because he had the Midas touch.

He'd had six hits in a row. *Pee-wee's Big Adventure*, *Beetlejuice*, *Batman*, *Edward Scissorhands*, *Batman Returns*, and *Nightmare Before Christmas*. Up to that time, only one other person had ever had six hits in a row.

MP: Who was that?

JG: Preston Sturges. *The Great McGinty*, *Christmas in July*, *The Lady Eve*, *Sullivan's Travels*, *Palm Beach Story*, *The Miracle of Morgan's Creek*, and *Hail the Conquering Hero*. Hang about, that's seven. Seven hits in a row. So, Preston Sturges did one better than Tim. But nobody had had six hits in a row in recent times. Not Steven Spielberg, not anybody. So, Tim was, at that time, the hottest director in Hollywood. Everything he did was of intense interest to everybody.

And no one was developing science fiction movies. With the exception of *Star Trek*, which had a fan-base. The dogma was that sci-fi movies were like Westerns. They lost money. Nobody wanted to see them. The last hit sci-fi movie, apart from *Star Trek*, was *Return of the Jedi*, and that was back in 1983.

So, when the Topps Company advertised that Tim Burton was planning a film called *Mars Attacks!* all the studios commissioned science fiction films. And someone got ahold of the first draft of my script, and copied it.

MP: Who copied it?

JG: *Independence Day*. And they copied it completely apart from the third act, which they totally changed, giving it a different ending. It was the same concept and even had some of the same characters. It was a disaster movie, with the same structure as *Mars Attacks!* but they changed the locations, most of them, and the style was different. It was a straight drama, not a comedy.

MP: Wow! Actually, I never saw that movie, I gotta watch it now to see that. So that was also about Martians?

JG: Yeah, yeah. It was a copy of *Mars Attacks!* They got the script. I don't know how. But I was so busy working with Tim, I didn't know anything about it. I had no idea another company was copying it.

MP: As it was being written?

JG: Yeah. They were fast-tracking it, so they could get it out before *Mars Attacks!* This happens a lot. Do you remember the two Christopher Columbus movies?

MP: No.

JG: Yeah, um, one was from Paramount. Called *1492*, directed by Ridley Scott. That was the better one. The other was a Warner Bros movie called, I think, *Christopher Columbus*, which had Marlon Brando playing Torquemada. It's like: "Oh, we're making a movie about Christopher Columbus." Then another studio thinks that's a good idea and tells their people to make a film about Christopher Columbus and rush it out before the first one, and clean up on the joint buzz. Usually, but not always, the second film doesn't perform as well as the first one because people don't wanna see another film about Christopher Columbus.

MP: I wouldn't want to see any film about Christopher Columbus.

JG: Hahaha! Me neither.

MP: So, how do you think they actually got hold of the script?

JG: Through an agent would be my guess.

MP: Right. So, they just have a friend who is an agent?

JG: Yeah. You've got agents everywhere. And they often owe each other favors. They can get hold of any script, unless you do what Woody Allen does, which is not show anybody anything ever!

MP: So how does he get the actors to see if they wanna be in the movie if he's not giving them the script?

JG: He send out 'sides.' They're called sides. So, if he's looking for an actor, he'll get a scene which will be just a coupla pages and he'll send that out.

MP: But, if it's Woody Allen, I think people would wanna do it, whatever it is.

JG: Well, they do. But what he sends out... he's careful not to put in any jokes or anything like that. He just gives them a page that shows the character, so the actor has an idea of it. And the actor comes in and maybe does a reading.

MP: So, when Tim found out that they stole the script, was he disappointed?

JG: Well, yes, but there was nothing he could do. Nobody wants to take legal action because all the money goes to the lawyers, and you might get injunctions, which can stop the movie being released. We talked about it but there was nothing to be done. They didn't even change some of the names!

In the first draft, I had a character called Tiffany, who was a hooker. Her part was cut down in subsequent drafts, but she's in *Mars Attacks!* played by Rebecca Broussard. And her name was Tiffany. And, in *Independence Day* they had the same prostitutes and the main one was called Tiffany!

MP: Wow!

JG: They didn't even change her name! Hahaha! That kind of shows you how confident they were that nothing would happen to them.

MP: Wow!

JG: But they got *Independence Day* out before *Mars Attacks!* in the summer. Actually, they released it about three weeks before the original release date of *Mars Attacks!* So, you can see the whole thing was planned, and they knew what they were doing. And, *Independence Day* did very well. It had a great release campaign and was very successful. More successful than *Mars Attacks!* which, because of the delays, came out six months later, at Christmas. So, there it is. That's plagiarism for you...

MP: Wow, and it happens a lot?

JG: Happens a lot. Happened to me with another project called *Frankenstein*. That was a... That was for Paula Weinstein. Spring Creek Productions. She was the producer. I went to her office – sent down there by my agent for a meeting. And she was sitting in her office. Beautiful woman. I'd heard about her because I had a friend, a movie producer in London, called

Sandy Lieberson who was in love with her. Anyway, she had this nice office with flowers and everything, and a picture of Marlon Brando on the wall. I remember her telling me some funny stories about him. And I was impressed that she knew him because he's my hero. Best actor ever. And then she said: "So, Jonathan, what would you like to do for us?"

I said: "Well, I don't know. I haven't got anything!"

She said: "Well, we have a list of projects here. Have a look through and pick one you like."

There were about twelve projects and one of them was *Frankenstein*. I didn't like any of the other ones, so I said: "I like Frankenstein."

And she said: "How would you do it?"

And I said: "Well Paula, the thing about *Frankenstein* is it's never really been done." The old Universal movies, which were done in the 30's, they weren't really based on the book. And, if you read the book, Mary Shelley's *Frankenstein*, it's really an interesting book. It's actually very moving. But really what it's about, essentially, is it's about a mother and her child. But it's written so the child is actually created by a man. And the man isn't maternal. So, then there's this rejection of the child, and this withholding and withdrawing of love is traumatizing. It's child abuse. And the abuse makes the child become a monster. So, it's all to do with the cruelty of the parent. Dr. Frankenstein is a cold, cruel, narcissistic father, and the monster is a child who's been traumatized. So, the monster is actually a very sympathetic character.

MP: I remember reading it, *Mary Shelley's Frankenstein*, your screenplay, several times. It made me cry. It was so beautiful. It just added humanity to this character. It was just so lovely.

JG: Thank you. It was a different thing for me to do because it wasn't a comedy. I wanted to see if I could do something like that. And I was proud of that script. Pam really liked it, my mother. She said: "Oh, I didn't know you could write like this!" Because it's very emotional and dramatic, and yes, it's very sad.

MP: Yeah, it would have been a wonderful movie...

JG: But I blew it. It was all my fault. I made a mistake because I was stupid, stupid, stupid! I was at a party, and this guy, a friend of mine, asked me: "What are you doing at the moment?" Now, normally, you never, ever tell anyone what you're doing. It's one of the golden rules in Hollywood. But this was a friend I'd known for some time, and he was my neighbor, and he was a buddy, and he was very friendly, and I trusted him. So, I said: "Oh, I'm doing *Frankenstein*." And he said: "How are you doing it?" And, of course I was inspired, you see, at the time. I was in the middle of writing it, and high on it. So, I said: "Well, nobody's ever done it before. It's a romantic tragedy. The monster is really a very sympathetic character. What I'm doing is the book, and I'm calling it *Mary Wollstoncraft Shelley's Frankenstein*. It's not the Frankenstein we're used to. It's Mary Wollstoncraft Shelley's Frankenstein."

This guy, my friend, was working with a producer at the time, and he got fired. So, he didn't have a job. So, he was looking for a job and he went to a studio – I think it was Sony – for a job interview, and he, I believe, told the guys at Sony this idea and said that Tim Burton's writer was doing it and blah blah blah. And Sony had just done *Dracula* with Gary Oldman and Tony Hopkins, and they were tight with Coppola, who'd directed it, and they thought: "Oh, we'll do

77

it, and get Coppola to put his name on it as a producer to give people confidence so they'll say yes to the film." So, they got *Frankenstein* going straight away. Fast-tracked it.

I was writing the script. I don't mean just one draft, I mean I went through it four times and, by the time I was done, Paula, the producer said: "We're not doing it because they're doing it over at Sony."

MP: Did she know they'd stolen it?

JG: Oh yeah. And she was very, very angry about it. Because, I mean, they paid me good money for it. And they liked my script. Paula Weinstein wanted to do it. She… I didn't… I didn't tell her that it was my fault. Me and my big mouth. I never told her that. If Paula reads this, she's gonna hate me!

MP: Yeah, but you thought this was your friend, huh? Now, that teaches you not to tell even your friends.

JG: Yeah, I learnt my lesson there. So, Sony made the movie and they called it *Mary Shelley's Frankenstein*. They took out the Wollstonecraft. I liked the Wollstonecraft! I thought it made the title special. But they cut it out. But, so, yeah, anyway plagiarism is something that happens a lot. You have to guard against it, and there are many, many stories like that.

MP: Well, all right, so that's plagiarism. Now, what about credits? I wanted to ask you how the credit thing works.

JG: What, on *Mars Attacks!*?

MP: Yes. And in general.

JG: Well, that's very... That can be a big can of worms. You see, it used to be that whoever had the power... If it was, say, Charlie Chaplin; if he was doing a film for United Artists, say, he was the boss. He was the producer, the director and the star. Plus, he was one of the partners in United Artists. So, he could give himself the writing credit. And that kind of thing went on all the time! But, fortunately, we got the Writers Guild of America which is a fantastic organization. I mean, we'd all be sunk without it. And they fought many, many battles over the years, and they forced the studios to have a fair, independent system for the apportioning of credits.

See, each studio makes about twelve films a year, and those films are shown all over the world, and they make hundreds of millions of dollars, okay? And there's eight hundred thousand people in the movie industry and they all want a piece of the pie. They all want to be part of it, right? So, when there's a big movie, like *Mars Attacks!* for example, people try to get their names on it. Because it's good for their reputation, good for business.

Now, as you know, we had a couple of guys, Scott and Larry, who did two drafts of *Mars Attacks!* I first met them, I think, on *Ed Wood*. They wrote the screenplay. And they were nice guys. Larry was the one I really got to know. I didn't get to know Scott. He was more introverted. They were a writing team.

You get lots of writing teams in Hollywood. Usually one guy does most of the writing, and the other guy does the hustling.

Anyway, I chatted to Larry Karazewski quite a few times. And, when I was fired from *Mars Attacks!* I suggested they take over. I thought they'd do a good job, and protect the integrity of the script. But, for some reason, in this case, they didn't. Although they did put in some nice gags.

My favorite was during the scene with the prostitutes. One of them says to Tiffany, played by Rebecca Broussard: "Would you do it with a Martian?" And Tiffany says: "Yes, but no kissing on the lips!"

I don't know why Tim cut that. But there would have been a good reason. Maybe they needed to cut it to get a PG-13 rating? I don't know.

Anyway, Scott and Larry are good, professional screenwriters, and naturally they wanted a writing credit. Now, I don't know what happened between them and the Creative Team at the studio, so, I can't speculate. But what they did was change the whole of the third act. They changed it so much that, if there was a Writers Guild arbitration, they would most likely get a writing credit. The Writers Guild would see they'd made a major contribution and award them a co-credit.

But, when the script got kicked back to me again, I took out what they did. I only kept a few bits and pieces of what they did. So, the credit was 'Screenplay by Jonathan Gems,' right? But they challenged it and it went to the Writers Guild.

It was worth them trying because you never know, they might have gotten lucky. And if they'd been awarded shared credit with me, they would have had half the residuals.

So, I had to go through an arbitration process, and prove to the Writers Guild of America how much of the script I'd done – which was well over 90%.

Luckily, I'd kept my drafts, about fourteen of them. The interesting thing is final drafts are always an even number, like six or eight. If you're delivering, say the fifth or the seventh draft and telling them it's finished, you're wrong. It's not finished. The finished script is always an even number.

MP: Why is that?

JG: Because of the two sides of the brain. Your first draft, you're being creative. You're second draft is a critical response to your first draft. So, if you do a third draft, you're adding new stuff. You're being creative again. So, then, to polish it, you need a fourth draft, where you're refining the material.

So, anyway, I sent copies of all the drafts in, plus I'd written the book as well, so I sent that in too. And then I wrote a statement saying why I thought I should have sole credit, explaining what had happened and everything else. And the arbitration panel, they did the investigation. And then they had a hearing, like a court, and they voted to give me sole credit.

MP: Wow! You helped them by getting them the job, and then they turn around and try to nick your credit!

JG: Yeah, well. But that's Hollywood. I never felt any animosity toward Scott and Larry. I mean, it was worth them trying. And that's how things work in Los Angeles. Everyone's out for themselves. You have to be. It's the law of the land. And if you're not like that, if you do things that are altruistic, they look at you like you've lost your marbles. Or, more often, they're suspicious. They wonder what your game is.

I remember being offered a job by the producer Scott Rudin. He asked me to write *The Addams Family*, based on the TV series. I was put up for it by Lisa Henson, a great young executive I'd met on *Batman*. She was a D-girl at

Warner Bros and, later, she became president of Columbia Pictures. Very smart.

Anyway, she recommended me to Scott Rudin and I watched some of the TV episodes, and I thought I was wrong for it. I liked *The Addams Family*, and I remember thinking it had a good part for Anjelica Huston, who was a friend of mine – we'd gone to school together – but I didn't feel confident about doing it. It wasn't my cup of tea and, even though I liked Scott Rudin, and wanted to please Lisa Henson, I couldn't do it.

You know, to write a script, it takes a lot out of you, and you need to be inspired. I once made the mistake of writing a script because I needed the money, and it was a horrible experience. I was really ashamed of myself. Never again!

So, not wanting to disappoint Scott and Lisa Henson too much, I thought of someone who *could* write the screenplay. Caroline Thompson. I'd first met her in 1988, on a trip to L.A. when Tim Burton was still in London, finishing off *Batman*. He gave me her number and told me to look her up. She was a friend of his, and working on the script that became *Edward Scissorhands*.

And she was kind to me. She drove me around, showing me the sights. And, of course, *Edward Scissorhands* was a lovely script. So, I went into this meeting with Scott Rudin and Lisa Henson and I said: "I've got good news and bad news. What do you want first?"

Scott said: "Let's hear the bad news first."

So, I said: "I'm not writing the movie."

"So, what's the good news?"

"The good news is I've got a writer for you who's perfect for it."

"Who's that?"

"Caroline Thompson."

So, she got the job, and everything turned out well. Also, Anjelica, who I'd suggested for Morticia, got the part and was brilliant in it. So, it turned out great for everyone. But the next time I saw Caroline, she gave me the cold shoulder. She was very frosty. In fact, she was never nice to me again after that.

Altruism is not understood in L.A. You see, everything is quid pro quo. I do you a favor, you do me a favor. If you help someone, they think you're trying to get them in your debt. They think you're working an angle on them. And they don't like it.

MP: So, it's really a back-to-front code of ethics?

JG: I guess you could say that. It's an ethic based on the belief that everyone is selfish, which, in a way, is pragmatic. It's a business ethic. Everything is an exchange.

So, what were we talking about? Ah yes, credits! Well, in my experience, the whole credit thing's been rather patchy. The first feature film I wrote was *George Orwell's 1984*. Now, the story behind that was: I was given a script by Mike Radford, the director. He said: "I've written this script, based on the book by George Orwell, have a read of it."

So, I read it, and well, I didn't think it was very good. But I was a playwright. I wasn't a screenwriter then. So, I probably wasn't a good judge. So, when I spoke to Mike Radford, I didn't tell him what I really thought. But I did point out a few things, small things, a few obvious weaknesses, you know. And he went ballistic. He said: "Seven other people have read this script and they all say it's brilliant! You don't know what you're talking about!"

So, I thought: "That's the last time I hear from *him!*"

But, to my complete surprise, two weeks later, he calls me and says: "Are you free at the moment? 'Cause I'm in a pub down the road from you, and I was wondering if you've got time for a drink?"

So, I go down to this little pub in Portobello Road, and he asked me to rewrite the script. And that says a lot about Mike, that he didn't listen to his yes-men and, after thinking about it, decided to offer me the rewrite. I was very surprised.

So, I rewrote it and got along so well with Mike that he asked me to be his assistant during the shoot. And this was a great thing for me, for which I'll always be grateful, because it was an education. An education in filmmaking.

I worked with Mike every day on that film and, when the shoot was over, Mike fell ill, so I was deputed to stand in for him during post-production, and I worked on the editing with Tom Priestley, the editor, and wrote voice-over dialogue, which we had John Hurt come in and record, and so on.

Anyway, at the wrap party at the Groucho Club, organized by Simon Perry, the producer, a funny thing happened. I was in a booth, kind of trying to deal with being drunk, and a guy sat down opposite me, and we started talking. I hadn't seen the guy before, so I was wondering what he'd done on the film. So, I said: "What did you do on the film?"

And he said: "I wrote it."

And I said: "What do you mean you wrote it?"

And he said: "Well, I wrote the script."

"What's your name?"

He said his name was Antonio, or it might have been Eduardo, and I think he said he was from Argentina. He was a film student.

"So, you wrote it?" I said.

"Yes," he said. "Mike was very kind to me. He gave me some money to adapt the book and it was a very good experience for me."

I remember he smiled a lot. He seemed like a nice, happy guy. Or perhaps he was stoned. He was quite young, younger than me, with thick, curly brown hair and white teeth. He told me he was studying screenwriting, and had agreed to give Mike the writing credit because he was only a student."

Now, I don't know if what he said was true. I never saw him again, and I never dared ask Mike about it. But you see? The script that Mike handed to me had *Nineteen Eighty-Four by Mike Radford* on it. But, probably, it had been written by this Argentinian student.

And then Mike did the same thing to me. He persuaded me I didn't need a writing credit because I was a playwright. I wasn't in the film business. It meant nothing to me. But it was important for him because he could attract more work as a writer/director than as just a director. And, of course, I liked Mike and was very grateful to him. Also, I was on salary for the whole film, so I was well paid.

MP: And then he put his name to it?

JG: Yeah.

MP: So, how would you deal with that now? Just a quick question. If that happened to you now, and somebody said: "You don't need the credit." What would you say?

JG: Well, I'd tell them to take a running jump. Haha! Yeah, but I was young and I didn't know anything. But, I had a good agent, called Judy Daish, and when she found out about this, she went on the warpath. She said: "This is wrong. You should have a credit." And I was saying: "No, no, it's fine. I don't need a credit. I agreed with Mike he could have it." But she ignored me and, behind my back, she went to the producer, Simon Perry, and got me a credit. But it wasn't a front credit. It was a back credit.

MP: Oh, I forgot. Does it say: 'Screenplay by Jonathan Gems'?

JG: No, it says: 'Additional script material by Jonathan Gems.' And it's at the back, not the front. Hahaha!

MP: Well, I suppose that's something. Do you get any royalties from that?

JG: Oh no! I was so green back then. I didn't know about royalties. You have to have a front credit for that. So, it was a way of crediting me without having to pay me any money!

MP: Oh!

(Both laugh heartily.)

MP: So, any other movies like that?

JG: Yeah. *White Mischief*, also directed by Mike Radford. He gave himself a co-writing credit on that one. At least, this time, he let me share it. Hahaha!

MP: Didn't you work on some of Tim Burton's films?

JG: In a way, but not enough to deserve a credit. I was like Tim's consigliore. In France, they call it a "neige."

MP: Like "snow"?

JG: Yeah. I don't know why they call it snow. But it's like the person you bounce your ideas off. And I would read the scripts Tim was offered. And sometimes books. You know, whatever was coming down the pike. He'd say: "Have a look at this, and tell me what you think."

I remember once his agent was putting a lot of pressure on him to do a movie based on a book called *Mary Reilly*. He got me to read it, and I said: "Don't do it." So, he didn't do it.

And when he was doing a picture, he often liked to talk to me about it. Casting, especially. And I was his unofficial script guy. He would get my input on the scripts he was doing, and we'd discuss them, and make changes.

On all his films, Tim would have ideas to incorporate into the script, so I helped him with that. So, we would discuss it all, and put those things in and make a few cuts. That happened on *Ed Wood* and *Edward Scissorhands*. Not on *Batman 2* though. I was in New York when he was doing that.

MP: Were you present during the filming of them?

JG: Well, I popped down to the set a few times...

MP: Tim Burton strikes me as totally not a greedy person. He's somebody who's fair.

JG: Absolutely. He's fair to everybody. He doesn't have that sort of ego that some people have, like David Cameron or somebody, where they want to own everything.

MP: He strikes me as – when you describe him to me – as a true artist. He cares about the movie; that the movie is going to be good. He doesn't get caught up in all that ego stuff.

JG: That's exactly right. He knows that the ego, although you need it, can be an obstacle. It's a tricky balance. You need a strong ego to create things and put them out there and stick up for yourself. But, at the same time, if you don't restrain your ego, you can wreck everything. What some artists do, to help with this problem, is give it all to God. God is the creator. God has created you, and anything good you do, it's not really you, it's God working through you. So, don't get big-headed about it!

MP: So, how was it filming *Mars Attacks!*?

JG: Well, it was all a bit mad. People were being cool but, underneath, there was a kind of frenzy. We were under a time crunch the whole time, so, you know... I haven't really thought about it, but I just remember what a funny bunch of people they were. I mean, a real rag-tag bunch of weirdos. It was like being in a traveling freak show. Hahaha!

MP: Hahaha! It must have been fun.

JG: Hahaha! It was different. It wasn't one of those films, like *White Mischief*,* where you have a small group doing the main parts. *Mars Attacks!* wasn't like that. It was so crazy. So big. There were so many actors. We had about two hundred people on the crew, and they were building these big sets, and there was always a lot of activity going on around you. There wasn't time to really connect with anyone. The actors would come in, do their bit, and go. Everybody was so busy and rushing off...

---

* Starring Charles Dance, Greta Scacchi, John Hurt and Joss Ackland, directed by Michael Radford.

MP: To other projects?

JG: Well, not that necessarily. There just wasn't a lot of time. And it was the nature of the film. We had such a big cast. I mean, the biggest role was Jack Nicholson as the president, but it wasn't like the movie was about him. There were lots of different stories going on. There were lots of people on the film, coming and going. It felt like Heathrow Airport.

MP: Really? Wow.

JG: Yeah. I met and chatted to some of the guys on the crew, and some of the actors, but only briefly. It wasn't a leisurely shoot where you could hang out. And it was a bit nerve-wracking for me because, when you're the writer, you can't talk to the actors too much, because… because it undermines the director. Actors, sometimes, some actors, they can be kind of needy. They've got lots of questions about the character, and they can kind of jump on you. You know, like: "So, what is he thinking here? Why does he put it this way and not another way?" Or, "I don't understand this line, I'd rather say it like this." Sometimes they want you to give them more lines. They want you to expand their part.

But the trouble is, if you get too involved – and it's tempting to do it – you undermine the director. The actors, and the movie, benefit the most by having one person direct it, and that's the director. So, I would talk to Tim, but restrict what I said to everyone else. If you don't do that, what happens is, when they're shooting a scene and the director says: "Oh, can you try it like this?" The actor might say: "Well, I just spoke to the writer and he says *this* is the way to do it."

MP: Ah, okay, okay. So, yeah, so, you would need to politely, kind of…

JG: I had to keep myself in check. I couldn't get into it with the actors. I mean, I would have loved to. I'm sure every writer wants to. But you're not the director, so you can't. But I remember Natalie Portman, for example. She was very young, and she seemed very tense and shy. No one was talking to her, and she appeared to be lonely and abandoned in the middle of this storm that was going on around her. So, I tried to cheer her up. But it didn't work. She was very reserved.

And then I realized she was method-acting. Her character in the movie was isolated. No one paid her any attention. She was lonely and abandoned. And the storm of the filmmaking going on around us was like the storm that was going on around her character in the movie, with the Martians causing chaos and everything. She was using it, you see? Clever. A very clever actress. And she was so young. She was a child prodigy.

One thing though… She asked me what her character was reading. What books was she reading? And I said *Siddartha*, by Hermann Hesse, because her character was an intelligent girl seeking truth in a world of lies. And, you know, *Siddartha* is about the Buddha…

MP: Yes, I noticed that. Did you talk to Jack Nicholson?

JG: Yeah. But not much on the movie. He came over to me once, and said: "Hey buddy, we need some lines here." He was playing… One of his parts was Art, the Texas billionaire, who owned the Galaxy Hotel, and he wanted some new lines for a scene with his wife, played by Annette Bening. He knew what he needed but didn't know what the lines should be.

So, I tried to understand him, and write some dialogue, but everything I came up with, he didn't like. He knew the scene needed something, and he was right about that. And we both saw it was an opportunity to reveal the character of Art Land, which he was busy concocting. So, we went through a back and forth process and, finally, he nodded his head, then went away and wrote the dialogue himself. And came up with the idea of taking off his wig. Working with him was like working with a speedy chef – you know, stirring pots and throwing in all kinds of different herbs and vegetables at a high rate of speed.

Tom Jones was the opposite. Very serene. He had that body-builder thing. You know how body-builders are relaxed? There was this strong, quiet warmth about him. Everybody liked him. He wasn't an actor. He was a regular guy. An oasis of sanity in a raging sea of actors, which was the *Mars Attacks!* set. But, of course he *was* an actor. He was acting all the time!

MP: What do you mean?

JG: He was acting Tom Jones!

You know, I sometimes got the feeling that a lot of the stars in the film were uneasy about doing it. Actors pick everything up. They are very sensitive to vibes. And there were waves of anxiety coming from the studio. So, I guess they were picking up on that. And I think… I think some of them didn't entirely get the script. And the reason they were doing it was really because of Tim Burton and Jack Nicholson.

I remember thinking, when I watched scenes being shot, how brave the actors were. They weren't completely sure about what they were being asked to do, but they totally went for it. I mean, it could have all gone horribly wrong.

They could have all fallen flat on their faces. The film could have been a disaster. A disaster movie that was a disaster. Can you imagine the reviews? They'd love to say that! Mind you, there were people at Warner Bros who were *sure* it was gonna be a disaster!

See, what most actors like is a good role with layers, with light and shade, where they can be noble or fascinating, and where the character has a journey, an arc. And they like the challenge of expressing emotions in true and subtle ways. A role like *Erin Brockovich*, you know what I mean? But, in *Mars Attacks!* I mean, these characters were absurd.

MP: So, they weren't very attractive to actors?

JG: Right. Although Pierce Brosnan liked it. He was cast early. He liked the script and took to it like a duck to water. And he really enjoyed doing it. You can see that in his performance. And he was terrific in every take. He's my favorite in the film. He nailed it 100%. And I loved the way everyone was surprised to see James Bond as a misguided, mild-mannered science professor!

MP: Oh yes, that's true.

JG: My angle on the casting was to cast straight actors rather than comic actors because, in disaster movies, the actors are very serious and emotional because they're in a disaster, and disasters are very serious! And that's what makes it funny.

I liked Jerzy Skolimowski, who played the expert with the translating machine, because he was so serious. He was cast by Jeanne McCarthy, the casting director, a great bit of casting. Spot on, perfect. And I liked Michael J. Fox and Sarah

Jessica Parker because they were playing it like they were in a drama, not a comedy. But Tim's approach was to mix it up. Some of it played straight, and some of it played for laughs.

You know, when you write a script, you always know what you want – exactly what you want – but you never usually get it. That's why films that you've written are so disappointing and hard to watch. Mind you, actors and directors feel the exact same way. Everybody's disappointed! Ha ha! But there are usually some good bits, where the actor has improved on what you've written – and those bits are delightful. You get a real kick out of them. Some actors will add things and make it better, like Rod Steiger did with his general. What he did with it was high drama and high comedy. When that happens, it's like a co-creation and then you just, you know, honor the actor for what they've done, and certain actors always do that, like Timothy Spall. He always does that. He always makes everything better. And, Fred Molina, he's another one.

MP: The guy in your film *The Treat*?

JG: Yeah, he's very good.

MP: What about Jack Black?

JG: He was brilliant! He wasn't well-known at the time but he had a good agent who pushed him. Tim wasn't sure at first, but when he started doing his scenes, he was very glad he cast him. His energy was unbelievable. And all of his scenes, he turbo-charged them. He was very good. Really funny. Did you know Leonardo DiCaprio was gonna be in it?

MP: Imagine that! All that cast, plus Leonardo DiCaprio.

JG: Yeah. He was gonna play Richie, the boy Lukas Haas played. But remember, we went over schedule, because of the puppets and everything. We were six months late, so Leo couldn't do it. He suggested Lukas Haas.

MP: He was great!

JG: He was very good, yes. He was exactly right. Wonderful. We were lucky to have him.

MP: And the general, what was his name?

JG: Which one, which general? Paul Winfield?

MP: Sorry, that guy... "We will win!" What's his name again?

JG: Rod Steiger. He almost got me in trouble. He kept wanting to talk to me about his character, and the scene... his big speech, when he's being shrunk.

You know, he was such a big star, in the old days, I mean. He was, when I was growing up. Rod Steiger was one of the biggest stars in the world, along with Elisabeth Taylor, Richard Burton, Marlon Brando and Marilyn Monroe. Rod Steiger was a very powerful, impressive actor. He did *On The Waterfront*, a film called *The Pawnbroker* where he was amazing. I mean lots of films he did. *The Loved One*, written by one of my favorite writers, Terry Southern. *Doctor Zhivago*, which was a big movie when I was a kid, written by Robert Bolt, who was a friend of my mother's.

I used to look up to Bob Bolt. I really admired him. I wanted him to be my father.

And there he was, Rod Steiger. And he was playing a

part I wrote. It was hard to believe. I was a little scared of him, 'cause he looks like he's made out of igneous rock. It's funny how some people look like that, like they're on Mount Rushmore. I'll tell you someone else like that. George Harrison. He was taller than you think, bigger, his face like a monument. And Rod Steiger was like that. And he'd been a movie star for fifty years, and he was talking to me as if we were equals. And he's saying: "I don't think he would say this. I think he would say something more like this…" And "Do you think it would be a good idea to change this, so he could then turn around and do that?"

He wanted me to rewrite his dialogue, and he explained to me why. He'd figured out the whole back-story of this general, General Decker. He'd created a whole history for the character. And this was happening as the lights were being set, and there were lots of people walking about, and people sort of running up and saying: "Oh, Mr. Steiger, we're ready for your fitting now!" "Mr. Steiger, can we get you into hair and make-up?" and "We need you to try this new shirt."

There's all this going on and he's like: "C'mon, c'mon!" And he made me go with him to his fitting, and carried on talking. And he was very intense about it. And I was kind of juggling it all in my head. "How I'm gonna handle this?" 'Cause I didn't want Tim to think I was interfering. But what could I do?

But the more he talked, the more I realized, even though I'd created the character, he knew more about him than I did. I'd thought a lot about General Decker. I'd based him partly on General Patton and my uncle, who was a Brigadier in the Paratroopers… but Steiger knew him inside-out. So, I had to defer to him. He was right. He was artistically right. On an artistic level, he outranked me!

So, we rewrote the speech and I went to clear it with Tim. But, actually, what happened was, Tim was so busy, I couldn't bust in and talk to him. And Steiger told him just before they were going to shoot it. And time was short, so Tim said: "Okay, try it." And I remember there were quite a few takes of that scene, and Steiger was really selling it. And it worked.

We talked about other things as well. I can't remember now, I mean, it was a long time ago. We talked about his films. He had a lot of energy, Steiger. He talked about *The Pawnbroker*. That was one of his favorite films. And he was very happy working. He was seventy, but he looked fifteen years younger, and he was totally at home on the movie set. He loved it. And all this talk we had, and fixing his dialogue, and talking about studio politics and his other films, that was fun for him. He was lovely.

MP: What about Michael J. Fox?

JG: Michael J. Fox was a dream. He was like your dream actor. Fluid. Effortless. Light as a feather. And a real sweetheart. I mean, one of the things was that there were so many actors. See, on most films, all the department heads get on with their jobs and the director looks after the actors. Well, Tim did some of that. He was close with Jack Nicholson, but he couldn't look after everybody, especially as he was more involved than most directors are with the nuts and bolts of filmmaking. He would get very involved in the set dressing for instance, and the costumes, the lighting – even specific gestures.

So, I would see these forlorn actors, well, they were stars – forlorn stars. They were so humble when they were working. You forgot they were stars. They were artists focused on what they were doing. And I think some of them would have liked more time to talk things over with Tim but he didn't have the time. And, sometimes, the actors would be called to the set but then they'd have to wait around. So, they'd sit there, waiting, kind of tense.

And I remember Michael J. Fox. He was sitting on the floor, in the corner, going over his lines. And, I had a chat with him and he was sweet. Very clear-minded. Mature for his age. He was young, but you got the feeling he'd been through a lot. He was pure and refined. A pure, refined spirit. And he had this bubbling, youthful energy.

We didn't know he had Parkinson's disease then. I don't think anybody knew. But I did notice there was pain in him. At the time, I wondered whether he'd had a tragic childhood, but it was probably coming from the Parkinson's. But, my God, he was a good actor!

You know, a lot of his stuff was cut, which was a pity. I guess it was a matter of balance and 'getting on with the story,' but it was a shame. If you read the script, there are scenes in there – his scenes – that we shot and he was superb in them. He was like a perfectly oiled acting machine. He could just do it. When Tim suggested something, Michael would just do it like that! (*snaps fingers*) And just nail it! Straight away. He was quick. Like a chameleon.

There are some actors who are like that. They have a facility for acting. And he was like that. I mean, I haven't done a lot of movies, and maybe it's more common than I'm aware of, but the only other actor I've met like Michael J. Fox, was Richard Burton. He was like that.

You know, you'd have a difficult scene, with lots of lines and business, and Richard Burton would do it, and then the director might say: "Oh, can we try it like this?" And Richard Burton would just do it instantly, and everyone would be stunned. It made the director nervous about making suggestions because Richard could instantly manifest them, which often showed everyone how dumb the suggestions were!

Michael J. Fox was the same. Everything he did was completely believable. I was so impressed by that. The only thing you might say about his work is… it could be a little too cerebral sometimes. And that was true of Richard Burton as well.

Sarah Jessica Parker was different; very emotional and intuitive. Michael was consistent; Sarah Jessica wasn't, which made them a great match-up in the movie. You know: "Men are from Mars, women are from Venus." Michael was masculine and logical; Sarah Jessica was feminine and emotional. Their different acting styles suited the characters they were playing. This is good casting.

Apart from the script, the most important thing in a movie is casting. Tim, no doubt because he's such a film buff and has studied thousands of movies, is very good at casting – usually. Although, there were three cases of miscasting in *Mars Attacks!* in my opinion. But we'll get on to that later. And, hey, three parts miscast out of thirty acting roles isn't bad.

Vicky Thomas and Jeanne McCarthy were the casting directors, and they were brilliant. And I liked them a lot because they got the script and were very gung-ho.

So, Sarah Jessica was great. I love how she acts. She does it from the inside out. She finds the soul of the character and then lets it take over. She had to play a ditzy TV presenter, which she did to perfection. And what I liked was, she would take chances. She would take a dive and sometimes it would be a flawless swallow dive, and sometimes it would be a noisy splash. Jack's like that, too. Fearless. That's what makes them exciting to watch. It's like watching someone on a high wire.

On the set, Sarah Jessica was nervous but, again, she was inhabiting the character, Nathalie, who was kind of brittle and nervous. So, she was being Nathalie.

I first met Sarah Jessica on *Ed Wood*, when Tim was making that. I'd suggested her for the role of Ed Wood's girlfriend, and Tim cast her. She was wonderfully funny in that. Very subtle and understated. She's one of the best actresses in America. As a person, she's not like the roles she plays. She's a New Yorker. Very sophisticated, clever, cultured, knowledgeable. One of Nature's aristocrats, like Angela Bassett or Trudie Styler. Very sophisticated and charming.

Who else was in it? Oh, oh yes. Glenn Close. I love her name, don't you? It sounds like a road. Well, she was… Everybody was impressed by her. She came in… she'd been in make-up for quite a while, and they'd got the look. She came in like the First Lady and everybody was laughing. And she did it straight off. I think they did most of her scenes in only a few takes – most of them. She was only there for six days. Super professional.

MP: What do you mean by super professional?

JG: Well, she just came in, ready. She had her lines; she looked perfect; she hit her marks. She knew where the lights were; she knew where the camera was; she knew everything. And she just did it, like, perfectly, you know? And she wasn't bothered by… There's a hell of a lot of distraction going on when you're making a film. And she didn't get distracted. Her focus, her concentration was 100%. She played the First Lady with this kind of self-conscious grace that was very funny. And she was very professional with the other actors.

MP: Wow! In what way?

JG: I mean, Jack Nicholson was spinning and sparking all over the place…

MP: Hahahaha!

JG: Letting it rip and improvising. That was his approach to this show – a little bit like how he was on *Batman*. So, he was inventing all kinds of wild stuff. He gave the crew a lot of laughs. But Glenn, Glenn she held the center. She was like his straight man. They must have worked this out together, and it worked very well. They were like Stan and Ollie. Glenn Close's First Lady was hilarious.

MP: Yeah! Perfect for the First Lady and the President!

JG: Yeah, and when she was there, she really was like a First Lady. Like the president of the student council, or the head girl. She kind of kept her eye on things, made sure everybody was okay. It was nice.

See, quite often, on a movie, you get the father of the cast. Sometimes, if the lead actor is a woman, she's the mother of the cast. That's what Glenn, very briefly, was: the mother of the cast.

Jack Nicholson, because he had the biggest part, could have been the Daddy, and he's done that on other movies, like *The Two Jakes* for example, but he didn't do it on this one. He had a big role and he was doing a lot of creative work on it, and he's a nice guy – a very warm, fun-loving guy. But he couldn't look after all the other actors. He told me once he can't remember anyone's name. He said he could only remember the names of the people he knew before 1975.

MP: Wow! Hahahaha! Sweet!

JG: I met him multiple times. And he never remembered my name.

MP: But he remembered you?

JG: Yeah, but he didn't know what my name was.

MP: So, he was right about that...

JG: Yeah, I did question him about it once. We were skiing. He had a house in Aspen, Colorado. A nice house there, and he had a collection of Pre-Raphaelite paintings. Unbelievably beautiful paintings. He collected the Pre-Raphaelites. And I love the Pre-Raphaelites. I was quite envious. I thought: "My God, if I were a successful actor like him, this is what I would do." I mean, they're really hard to get. There's a limited number of them, and they're very expensive. But Jack started collecting them before they were fashionable so, some of them he got very cheap. To get even one is amazing! And he had more than a dozen – by Waterhouse, Rossetti, Millais, and Holman Hunt.

Anyhow, it was on that ski trip that I complained he couldn't remember my name. And he said, after he did *One Flew Over the Cuckoo's Nest*, he became famous and he was meeting about fifty people a week, and they were all telling him their names and this went on and on for years and his brain just said: "No."

MP: Wow.

JG: He just: "I'm not gonna bother remembering anybody's name anymore." Hahaha!

MP: Well, it must be difficult. Ahhh, so, anyway, so who else was in *Mars Attacks!*?

JG: Well there were lots of people. Let's see, there was Jim Brown, he was great. He was an amazing guy, Jim Brown. He played the boxer. And Annette Bening, she was great.

MP: What was Jim Brown like?

JG: Very interesting. He was like a philosopher and we had a couple of long talks. There wasn't much for me to say to him about his character, because it was based on Joe Louis, the champion boxer who lost all his money and got a job working as a greeter at Caesar's Palace. He knew that and that was all he needed to know. The character was originally Tim's idea. He suggested that character.

Jim Brown was a famous actor. As a kid, I loved him in *The Dirty Dozen*, and *Ice Station Zebra* and, later on, he was in a Keenan Ivory Wayans film called *I'm Gonna Git You Sucka,* which I liked. And before he was movie star, he was a famous football player. I think he was a fullback. One magazine voted him 'Best American Football Player Ever.' An extraordinary man. And what we talked about was… Well, it was about the prison system in America and the plight of young black men.

A very high proportion of young black men were in prison, and most young blacks would spend at least some time in prison. I remember we talked about *The Gulag Archipelago*, by Aleksandr Solzhenitsyn, and he gave me the history of how blacks were manipulated by political parties for votes, and how the CIA corrupted the young men with heroin and crack cocaine.

He was a fund of knowledge, and angry about how his fellow African Americans had been treated. But he wasn't bitter. He was like a college professor. Rational and pragmatic. He did a lot of work in prisons, talking to prisoners, trying to help them do their time, and believe in themselves and correct their problems.

He was the first person to tell me about what happened in the late 60's, which was when welfare was introduced to the black communities. This broke up most of the families because what the government did was give the welfare money to the mother, not the father. This displaced the fathers. The fathers lost their role and their status, so many of them split. They left. There were millions of divorces. Before welfare, the divorce rate in black families was lower than in white families. It was about 6%. Then it shot up to 68%.

MP: Wow.

JG: So, you had all these kids growing up with no fathers and this was especially bad for the boys, and most of them joined gangs and became delinquent. So, what Jim Brown was doing in these penitentiaries was, he was being a father to these boys that were in prison.

MP: Wow.

JG: Teaching them how to grow up and be a man. And he was a wonderful, wonderful guy; and a really important guy. He didn't really take the film too seriously. Ha ha! I mean, he was great in it, but a lot of the time he was on the phone, talking to his organization. He was running this whole nationwide organization doing charity work.

MP: Wow!

JG: Mainly for young black men in prison.

MP: That was his main interest?

JG: That's what he cared about. He wasn't into acting that much anymore. And he had all kinds of petitions going and, you know, working with different senators and congressmen, trying to get prison reform.

He did a lot of work for black communities. And he was very wise about it. He was the man who told me about the plantation system, and how that worked, and it was fascinating because it's actually the way our government still works today, in the UK. But that's another story. But, no, Jim Brown. He is magnificent. A great American. Like Martin Luther King.

MP: Wow! And he does look very... Something about his face. Like has a big heart. That's how he comes across on screen.

JG: Ah, really?

MP: Yeah.

JG: Well, it's true. He has a *huge* heart!

MP: And I didn't know whether it was because his character had a big heart or...

JG: It was him *and* the character. Both. That's why he was great casting. I've just remembered Jack rewrote some of the dialogue in the cab scene. You remember that scene? Jack and Jim Brown are in the cab together?

MP: Is that where he says he's given up pork?

JG: Yeah.

MP: And then Jack says: "You don't eat pork??" Hahahaha!

JG: Hahahaha, yeah. He improvised that bit.

MP: What about Danny DeVito?

JG: Yeah. Well, he was amazing. He took a small part and made it big. He's an amazing guy. He's like a human firework. It was very nice of him to come in and play the lawyer. He did it as a favor to Tim.

Remember the Penguin in *Batman Returns*? Incomparable. I really think his Penguin is one of the greatest movie creations ever. I was told he's a very good businessman – like Bob Hope was. Actors admire actors who are good at business because most of them aren't! They're like musicians in that way. He's clever. He wasn't on the movie long. Just a few days. He was sweet, warm, funny and friendly with everybody. He wanted to make the character more sympathetic, which Tim agreed with, and he created that character. It was his creation. I hadn't written it like that. Hahahaha!

MP: Ah, okay! Hahaha! When he offers the Martians the Rolex, and tells them: "If you wanna conquer the world, you're gonna need lawyers, right?" Hahaha! It's just great!

JG: Well, yeah, but when I wrote that, I saw it being played straight. You know how lawyers are. They're not charming and funny like Danny DeVito. They're kind of stiff, right? They have this papier-mâché dignity. And they're self-important. Donald Trump has a lawyer called Jay Seculow, who's been on TV recently. Like that. That's the type I was thinking of. You know, sharp suit, eagle-eyed, and talks like he's making a case.

MP: Right, right. But hahahaha! It was so cool what he did.

JG: Well, Danny DeVito, he played it... He played it more like a Mafia lawyer.

MP: Hahahaha! Yeah, yeah, he's like a Mafia lawyer.

JG: Yeah, but it was fine.

MP: It was a caricature, wasn't it? 'Cause they all pretend to be straight. He was showing what's underneath.

JG: That's right. You're right. He was doing the id of the lawyer, rather than the ego. Tim loved it. He loved what Danny did. And that's the main thing.

MP: It was great! I loved it. That's one of my favorite scenes. There are many, many scenes that are my favorite, but that one is so great! I love it. It's the essence. The essence of our materialistic way of life...

JG: The Rolex. The symbol of our value system. But he did it, and turned it into a comic turn. And this is how Tim directed the movie as a whole, and I think he was probably right now. At the time, I was worried. I remember when we were casting, because Tim was telling everyone it was a comedy, and I said: "Don't tell them it's a comedy!" I thought it should be played straight. I thought it would be funnier that way.

MP: Ohh. So, they overdid it. That actually is a bit visible.

JG: Yeah. I liked Pierce Brosnan because he played it straight. And that's why it's funny. And if Danny DeVito had played the lawyer like Jay Seculow, or one of those kind of lawyers, it would have been funny in a deeper way. Whereas, by clowning, it kind of trivializes it.

MP: Right. Yeah, yeah, I actually noticed that...

JG: Jack did that too when he played the billionaire. The Art Land character. He was clowning it. I wanted Ben Gazzara for that part. Have you seen *The Killing of a Chinese Bookie*? By John Cassavetes? I saw Art Land as a variation on that character. A kind of a lowlife criminal who's a cut above, who has some good qualities but is fundamentally a sleazebag. I wanted Art Land to be like Ben Gazzara in *Killing of a Chinese Bookie*, but rich and successful, and owning a flashy casino hotel in Vegas. And he's got himself a pretty, younger wife who was a whore but is now doing yoga, and concerned about the environment.

And, uh, actually, Tim sounded out Ben Gazzara. He sent him the script. And Gazzara was interested. He was living in Greece or Cyprus or somewhere, but willing to fly in to do it. But Jack wanted to play that part. I'm not sure if that was the right decision. But Tim was playing it more comic. And I think now, for lots of reasons, he was right to do that.

Under his direction, I saw the film evolving into something more in the vein of *Hellzapoppin*, or *Night at the Opera* by the Marx Brothers. He could have had the actors play it straight. That's how he directed *Ed Wood*. The humor would have been drier, and the movie probably wouldn't have been as successful. It would have been less like an acid trip.

I mean, the way Jack played the casino owner was so random! And when he took off his wig, and you could see clearly it was Jack Nicholson, it blew away all the conventions. The movie did that a lot, breaking conventions, which helped create the movie's surreal, nitrous oxide type atmosphere. You know: all bets are off – madness and mayhem.

That's what Tim did with *Mars Attacks!* What I wrote was a satire, but what he did was turn it into a kind of delirium. Uh, my way – playing it straight – well, it would have been witty, and with all of Tim's visual gags and ideas, it would have been great to watch – but it wouldn't have been so… euphoric.

One thing I can say is: Jack doing the movie was pivotal. He was a big influence. He pushed it in that direction too. In that sense, he *was* the Daddy of the picture. Because some of the other actors took their cue from Jack. At one point, he was going to play three parts. Like Peter Sellers in *Dr. Strangelove*.

MP: Hahahaha!

JG: But he wound up doing two. Um, you know the War Room in *Dr. Strangelove*? Well, I copied it. The room with the maps, where the president and the generals are sitting around and deciding what to do? That was copied from *Dr. Strangelove*, hahaha! And Jack picked up on that, and he thought it would be fun to do what Peter Sellers did. So, he was gonna play the president, the billionaire, and the trailer-trash father, played by Joe Don Baker. But the schedule was too crazy.

MP: Actually, that guy was very good.

JG: He was. He's a superb actor. He's done a lot of great work. We were very lucky to get him. He was terrific.

MP: What about Martin Short?

JG: Well, Martin Short, I didn't meet him. I wasn't there when he was doing his scenes. I didn't want him for the part. I thought he was wrong for it.

MP: Oh, gosh I loved that part! I loved him! He's one of my favorites.

JG: Oh, really? Good, good. You see, it's hard for me to judge the film. If you like him, maybe he's good? The guy I wanted was Don Johnson. Do you remember Don Johnson? *Miami Vice*?

MP: Hahaha! Oh gosh, in Serbia, Yugoslavia, when we were kids, my mom was in love with him!

JG: Yeah, he was, he was fantastic. He was my ideal casting for…

MP: Oh, but I just love Martin Short! I don't know, I can't imagine anybody else doing it.

JG: Good, well, I'm happy, yeah. I mean, the reason Martin Short was cast… The funny thing is he was the first person cast in the movie.

MP: Really?

JG: Yeah. He did an imitation of Tim Burton on *Saturday Night Live*. Tim and Lisa-Marie watched it and Tim was inspired to offer him the press secretary. He was the first actor who was cast. And I was a bit taken aback. I'd worked with Tim on other films, and we'd always discuss the casting. I mean on *Edward Scissorhands* we had lots of long discussions before Johnny Depp got the part.

I mean, really… I mean, about 80% of directing a film is the casting. It's the most important thing. And, if you cast it correctly, most of your problems are solved. There's not a lot for you to do. You've got the director of photography looking after the lighting and the filming; the production designer doing the sets; you've got your costume designer taking care of the costumes. I mean, you as the director still have to say: "Well, I prefer the red dress over the green dress." "I don't like that chandelier." That kind of thing. But, basically, that's all you have to do, if you've cast it correctly.

The actors will do it, and you just watch them and pick the best take. Maybe you tweak it a bit. Faster, slower. "Let's try it another way," or whatever. But, if you *don't* cast it right, you have your work cut out. 'Cause you have to fix the problems caused by the miscasting.

We had that on another movie I wrote called *White Mischief*. One of the actresses was miscast. And she knew it too. She was marching around saying: "Who put me in this? I'm totally miscast!" We had to cut most of the movie's subplot because of that, which was a major loss. And the actress wasn't happy. Not at all. Actors would rather not work than be miscast.

Of course, it's down to the actor to decide whether or not he or she is right for the part. So, the actress in *White Mischief* should have turned the part down. But she didn't realize it until she was out in Kenya shooting it.

Anyway, casting is vitally important, and you discuss it a lot. And I was Tim's sounding board. So, he would discuss the casting with me, so then he would be armed, to talk about it, 'cause he'd have all his ideas and reasons ready. I mean, when it comes to casting, you're dealing with executives, agents, all kinds of people. And a lot of them want to cast their friends, or people they're trying to make deals with on other projects. Everybody's trying to get themselves or their pals in the movie. It's a minefield. You can make a lot of enemies. So, your mind needs to be clear about what you want and why, so people understand, and forgive you for not casting them.

So, that's why it's handy to have a sounding board – a buddy you can talk to – and go through all the actors, all the pros and cons. And that's what we did. But we never discussed Martin Short.

He may have discussed him with Lisa-Marie but not with me. And that was significant. That was the beginning. The beginning of the end for me. Because he was cutting me loose. This is the separation that happens between a writer and a director, and it's always painful. See, you've been working for months with this guy, creating this movie together, and you get very close. It's almost like a love affair.

But when the film is green-lit, the director has to switch gears. Now, he doesn't need you so much. The script is done. In fact, he doesn't even want you around, because he wants to do the rest of the movie himself. See, the creator of a film is the writer, but the realization of it is the director.

Anyhow, I'm glad you liked Martin Short, and I think most people do. So, it worked out. And I think his casting... the casting of Martin Short was kind of crucial. When Tim did that it was a marker. Martin Short was a comedian, you see? Tim had made up his mind to do the film as a comedy rather than a drama that's funny. If I'd been directing, I would have cast Don Johnson. For me, the press secretary was... I wanted a skirt-chaser, a shark, a ladies' man. I wanted Don Johnson playing a horn-dog.

MP: Uhuh?

JG: Yeah. That way, you would enjoy what happened between him and the Martian Girl, because he's this womanizer. And, if it was Don Johnson – a sexy, good-looking seducer – then, when his finger's bitten off...

MP: Martin Short is too intelligent for that?

JG: Well, no, it's not that. He's not a stud. He's not a lady-killer. He's not a sex machine.

MP: Oh God, I hope he doesn't read this book! He probably likes to be a sex machine!

JG: Well, he's not the type. He's like a will-o'-the-wisp. He's like – who's that character? Ahh, I don't know. What's his name? My brain's not working. Ariel! Ariel in *The Tempest*. A sprite. You know, a magical creature who flits about.

MP: Actually, Martin Short does seem a bit of a magical creature. Yeah, yeah. He could be a great Peter Pan.

JG: That's it! And Peter Pan's not a sex machine, is he?

MP: Yeah, but I really liked him. He really stuck in my mind. He's so delightful. The way he's fishing to have sex. You can see it on his face, and his gestures are so funny. He lights me up. He's got these landmark expressions, which I look forward to whenever I watch the film.

JG: Oh really?

MP: Yes. I didn't know Martin Short before seeing *Mars Attacks!* After that, I checked out other things he'd done and he's very funny. Actually, funnier than he is in *Mars Attacks!* But, for me, he was... I can't imagine anyone else doing it better.

JG: Well, that's good. He's a clever, inventive actor, no doubt about that. And Tim was very happy with him.

MP: Right, right. So, Annette Bening. What was she like?

JG: I only talked to her once, so I can't really say. She was lovely. Very charming. Adorable. The sort of girl you want to marry. An actress through and through. A real actress. What can I say? A quintessential actress.

MP: What about the people that worked on the set? You know, the lighting people and all the crew and everything?

JG: Well, that's all a bit… Let me think. That aspect of it, the grips and drivers, and the catering people, the riggers, the set dressers and everything, well, it's all a bit like a war. Some of the terms they use come from the military. From the army and navy. Which is appropriate because making a film is a bit like conducting a war. You have 'actions.' The director calls 'action.' You have your 'unit,' the film unit, first unit, second unit. You go on a 'recce.' You go on a 'shoot.' Crew, the term 'crew' is from the navy. Boom, a boom operator, a boom mike, that's from the navy too.

I can't say much about the crew because I wasn't on the shoot that much. I just popped down to the set, or the location, when I was needed. So, I didn't get to know the crew. But I remember, when Tim was shooting the Vegas scenes… I was there to do some rewrites. And we were going from location to location, with the crew and the actors. We were jumping into the van, going from one place to another, and it was all kind of hectic, right? But the crew were enjoying themselves. They were kind of exhilarated.

It was fun being in Vegas. And Peter Suchitsky, he was the D.P., the director of photography, so he was shooting it. And I hung out with him a little bit. He had a tough job, getting all the lighting organized. And Peter was working hard, shooting it all. People got impatient with him – but they always do with the D.P. 'Cause everybody wants to get on and do it, but they have to wait for the lights to be set up. You have to get the right color temperatures, the right atmosphere. You have to do all this stuff and it takes time. And so people were rushing and rushing and then having to screech to a halt and wait for Peter.

And Tim was incredible but he was under a lot of pressure, and I think he was sometimes a bit curt with Peter Suchitsky. They weren't very pally. And Peter was sensitive about that

I think. If he was, he shouldn't have been. Tim was curt with me too. And I understood why. He was under a lot of pressure.

There was another thing about Peter. He didn't flirt with the actors. He was very gentlemanly and professional and, of course, he's a great D.P. But actors are concerned about how they look onscreen and Peter wasn't an "Oh darling, you look wonderful!" type of guy. He was just focused on trying to give Tim what he wanted. And he did it too. The whole film looks great.

MP: Yeah! It's so bright and colorful.

JG: Although I didn't like the burning cows. But that wasn't Peter. That was the visual effects guys. I think it was Warner Digital that did that sequence. It should have been a lot better. A real, ground-shaking stampede, with more realistic flames, and lots of cuts. It could have been a real eye-popper, and it wasn't. They undersold it.

MP: I thought it was okay.

JG: I would have preferred it to be more violent and more shocking.

But costumes. That's part of the crew. We're talking about the crew, right? Well, Tim has this fantastic costume designer, Colleen Atwood. A very fetching young woman. Very attractive. She reminded me of my ex-girlfriend, Jean Seel, who was also a clothes designer. But Colleen was unaware of my admiration. I'd stand next to her, blushing, but she was totally oblivious. Not an inkling. Though she did look at me sometimes as if I was odd. Like, why was I always getting in her way?

There was only one time when she took any notice of me. I was wearing a padded, one-piece zip-up work-suit. I'd bought it in a hardware store in Upstate New York, and she was curious about it. It wasn't me she cared about, it was the work-suit!

She was very beautiful, Colleen, but unaware of her own beauty. She looked like the *Girl with a Pearl Earring* by Vermeer, only with dark hair. Or that painting of the *Lady with an Ermine* by Leonardo da Vinci. Colleen Atwood – sigh! She's a marvel. But all she cared about was clothes and her daughter.

I think she's the best costumier in Hollywood. Colleen Atwood. And, even though, it was difficult at times, like when we were in Kansas, shooting those scenes, she was there with rails of costumes, lots of alternatives, lots of spares, and I mean everything she came up with was fantastic. The clothes are brilliant.

MP: Really, really brilliant!

JG: She was always ahead of the game, and great with the actors. She has this sweet bedside manner, like a good doctor. Soothing. And I'm sure lots of guys fancied her, which is probably why she put up this protective shield.

MP: Did she have a boyfriend?

JG: I don't think so, no. But she was just great. She was to the crew what Annette Bening was to the cast – ideal wife-material.

INTERVIEW 3

MP: You know, one thing about *Mars Attacks!* It's the only one that seems to be half-Tim Burton and half something else. As if his other movies were all Tim Burton, but this one is different.

JG: I've heard other people say that too. But I don't agree. To me, it's totally a Tim Burton movie. Look at *Pee-wee's Big Adventure*, his first feature film. It's all kindergarten colors, just like *Mars Attacks!* And in *Nightmare Before Christmas*, you have Christmas World, which has the same color palette. And there it is again in *Charlie and the Chocolate Factory, Alice in Wonderland*, and *Dumbo*. You see it in *Edward Scissorhands* with the candy-colored suburban tract houses, and all those smiley housewives in colorful clothes. In *Beetlejuice,* you have a portrait of a happy couple in a cute, colorful American small town contrasted with the demonic underworld inhabited by Beetlejuice. But even the hell realm Beetlejuice comes from is portrayed in fairground colors.

What's so original in Tim Burton's movies is his up-ending of the dark/light paradigm. Normally, we think of sunshine as happiness and darkness as depression. We think of cute things as nice, and ugly things as nasty. But what we see in Tim's movies is that, well, life is more complex than that.

It's not that he's saying darkness and depression are good, not at all. But what he *is* saying is not to reject darkness and depression without seeing the truth and value in it. And he's also warning us that what is bright, cheerful and beautiful can also be evil and false. He probably developed this philosophy from working at Disney, hahaha!

And, look, most of his movies have demons in them, don't they? Like Beetlejuice is a demon, and Jack Skellington, the Joker, Sweeney Todd, the Headless Horseman, the Penguin... And *Mars Attacks!* has all these same elements. The hero in *Mars Attacks!* is Richie Norris, played by Lukas Haas, a young, disregarded son. The heroine is Taffy Dale, played by Natalie Portman, a young, undervalued daughter. Another heroine is Florence Norris, played by Sylvia Sidney, a neglected grand-mother, and another hero is Byron Williams, played by Jim Brown, a sad, downtrodden ex-boxer. These characters have all lived in a dark cave of depression. Barbara Land, the ex-drug addict yoga-bunny, also comes from a place of depression. Hence, the symbolism at the end of the film, when Barbara, Cindy, and Tom Jones emerge from a cave into the sunlight.

You can see parallels between Richie Norris, Ed Wood, Edward Scissorhands, Jack Skellington, and Batman. They are all characters fighting depression in a deceptive world full of demons. In *Mars Attacks!* the lesser demons are the human authority figures, and the cosmic demons are the Martians. It's totally a Tim Burton film.

MP: Yeah, I see what you mean. Maybe it's the satire? Maybe that's what's different?

JG: But there's satire in *Beetlejuice* and *Batman Returns*, and *Edward Scissorhands*...

MP: Yeah, yeah. So, it's not that. I don't know what it is. So, is there anything more you'd like to say about the casting?

JG: Well, casting, yes. When we were in pre-production, things were kind of fraught. Vicky and Jeannie were working long into the night, and it wasn't easy.

Tim wanted Warren Beatty to play the president. He was set on it. And it would have been funny having Warren Beatty do it. But the studio didn't want Warren. I think they'd had some kind of business dispute with him. I'm guessing it was one of those "You will never set foot in this studio again!" things. So, Tim couldn't have him, and he was very deflated by that.

Now, Jack Nicholson had always been my first choice for the president. But my vision of things wasn't the same as Tim's. Even though we'd worked together on the script, we didn't agree on everything, you know!

So, Tim was vacillating about the president, and Vicky and Jeannie were sending the script out to actors and they were all turning it down! The script was gaining a bad reputation, and Warner's said they were gonna cancel the film because nobody liked the script. Although Martin Short and Pierce Brosnan liked it. But they said they were gonna close the film down because we couldn't cast it.

Then Tim put feelers out to Jack's people and they told him he was unavailable. He wasn't reading scripts. He'd done a lot of work recently, and was taking some time off. But Tim got it to him somehow. And Jack read it, and he liked it, and said he'd do it. Jack saved the movie. He saved the movie because, when he said he'd do it, then all the other actors wanted to sign on.

MP: Oh, thank you Jack! Ohhhh!

JG: He liked the script. He told me that was the reason he did it.

MP: Ohhh, that's great...

JG: That was a special moment when he said that. I'd actually forgotten that until now. It was in Aspen. After the movie. He invited Tim up to Aspen. And we went – Tim, Lisa-Marie, and me, and we hung out at his house. We stayed for dinner. He had a fantastic cook, a black English guy from Liverpool. And we talked about a lot of things, and got a bit stoned, and that's when he told me.

MP: Not before?

JG: No, when we were making the movie he was always trying to change the script!

MP: Oh man, I really like Jack Nicholson.

JG: Yeah, he's something else. Amazing guy.

MP: I wish he lives a long, long time.

JG: Yeah,

MP: So, what's he like, Jack Nicholson?

JG: Very lovely, very intelligent. And a little bit crazy.

MP: In a good way?

JG: In a great way! Like, I remember us going up to the top of this mountain – way, way up this high mountain. On a ski lift. And we get to the top and there's nothing there except snow. Just snow everywhere, and there we were, above everything. There were clouds below us. You couldn't even see Aspen. And there was this freezing wind, and a little kind of hut on the summit, next to the ski lift. And I put my skis on, right? And he was on his skis, and we're on top of this freezing mountain. And there's this great slope that goes right down; this steep slope thick with snow, going down for about half a mile and disappearing into the clouds. And he had this cord around his neck, with a kind of capsule hanging on it. He opened this little capsule and, lo and behold, it had white powder in it. He put it on his thumb and took a sniff, through one nostril. Then sniffed some up the other nostril. Then he lifted his sticks and BOOM! He shot off the mountain!

MP: Hahahaha!

JG: He was going down the mountain like a bat out of hell. I was, like, "Fuck!"

MP: Hahahaha!

JG: So, I thought I'd better get going. So, off I went... But he was so far ahead of me, I never caught him. He was fifty-eight at the time, but he went down that mountain like a twenty-year old.

MP: The coke probably helped!

JG: Yeah. But, after Jack signed on, every actor in Hollywood wanted to be in the film. The biggest fans of actors are other actors. And Jack is like… well, like Brando used to be. Everyone wants to work with him. That's how we got such a good cast. And that was the last time the studio talked about canceling the film.

MP: And it did well, didn't it, after the receipts from Europe came in?

JG: Yeah, sure. I don't know what the worldwide gross was, the figures they put out aren't accurate, but it was more than three times the production cost. They made a profit, and the movie's been making profits ever since. And, for what it was, it was made very economically because the stars did it for scale. That is to say, union minimum. They didn't ask for their normal fees. I think Jack was the only one who got more than the minimum.

MP: Taurus, haha! He knows how to make deals.

JG: Yeah, he's done quite well out of Tim Burton. He made $60 million from *Batman*, Jack Nicholson. That was a lot of money in 1989; equivalent to, I'd say, at least $180million today. Because he got 14% of the gross. That was his deal. And, of course, that film was the highest grossing film in Warner Bros history up to that point. He probably spent the money on Pre-Raphaelite paintings!

MP: Hahaha! It's great! Haha! I mean what a character! But yeah, so you said the studio didn't advertise the movie well. Why was that, do you think?

JG: Well, that puzzled me for ages. The previews were great. The test scores were through the roof. But the executives were very shifty about it. They were shuffling around looking haunted. Why? I never found out. Maybe it was all the out-of-control screaming and yelling during the previews. They didn't understand it. *I* didn't understand it! It seemed like the studio didn't like the movie. And they did a poor campaign. Very lackluster. They didn't know how to sell it. I mean, we had about twenty stars!

MP: Really?

JG: Yeah! Nobody has twenty stars in a movie. Not these days. The last time that happened was in the thirties, when MGM could do it because they had so many stars under contract.

MP: I thought there were about five stars in *Mars Attacks!*

JG: No way! But I know why you think that. Because of how they advertised it. They only put five stars on the poster, which was an insult to the other stars actually.

After the film was done I was on the phone, and writing to Marketing and Distribution begging them… *begging* them to use the stars to sell the movie. All you needed was a poster with the title *Mars Attacks!* at the top, and pictures of all the stars looking worried, and the last picture being of a Martian. Who wouldn't want to see that? But they wouldn't talk to me.

MP: I don't think there's twenty stars.

JG: There are! Let's go through them. One: Jack Nicholson. Two: Danny DeVito. Three: Martin Short. Four: Annette

Bening. Five: Tom Jones. Six: Jack Black. Seven: Joe Don Baker. Eight: Lukas Haas. Nine: Sarah Jessica Parker. Ten: Rod Steiger. Eleven: Glenn Close. Twelve: Michael J. Fox. Thirteen: Pam Grier. Fourteen: Christina Applegate. Fifteen: Pierce Brosnan. Sixteen: Lisa-Marie. Seventeen: Jim Brown. Eighteen: Sylvia Sidney. Nineteen: Natalie Portman. Twenty: Paul Winfield. Twenty-one: O-Lan Jones.

MP: Oh, my God! Are they all stars?

JG: You bet. Some are bigger than others, but they're stars for sure. The only one on that list who hadn't had star billing on a movie was Lisa-Marie. And she deserved to be included, don't you think? Because she had a star part.

MP: Wow! You're right.

JG: The publicity department just threw it away. The worst publicity for a movie ever!

And the reviews were strange. When the first reviews came out, the first one I read was in *Hollywood Reporter*, and it was a rave. "This is fantastic. It's gonna be a smash." Then *Variety* came out, and that was a pan. And, after that, most of them were pans.

Much later, when I was in England, I met a film journalist, and I asked him about *Mars Attacks!* because he'd reviewed it for the *Evening Standard* newspaper. And I said to him: "You know, it was very odd to me – the reviews." Because, in the States, the *Hollywood Reporter* was a rave and there were a few other raves, but then the majority were negative but they didn't really say why. They didn't criticize anything specific. There were no reviews that said anything you could get your teeth into. Just a sort of general "Oh, it's not worth seeing" kind of thing. And I said to this reviewer: "Can you explain this to me?"

And he said: "We got the word that *Mars Attacks!* flopped in the States, and it was no good. So, that's how we wrote our reviews. But when it came out, and everybody loved it, then we realized we'd probably got it wrong."

He said he'd given the movie a bad review 'cause that's what everyone was saying. That was 'the word.' But after it was so popular, he wrote a second review saying he'd changed his mind, and the movie was good.

MP: Wow.

JG: So, you see, they were influenced. And it felt coordinated. So, I thought back to when the reviews came out in the States, and that felt coordinated too. They were all saying the same wishy-washy negative stuff. None of the critics said what the movie was really like. So, who was behind all this? Someone at the top was doing this.

It's a shock when you find out how coordinated the media is. Have you noticed how, on the news, all the stations are saying the same thing, even using the same exact phrases? And the newspapers. They lead with the same stories. And they'll have scare stories, almost every day, about climate change. It's a coordinated campaign.

This weirdness with the reviews woke me up to the fact that we really don't have a 'free press.' It's nearly all propaganda. And it's coordinated. And when I looked into it, I discovered that many people knew this. Books have been written about it, and what they call 'perception management.'

There's a hidden group of people – today, they call them

the Deep State – and these are the people behind the scenes who are running things. And they want us all to think alike. They use the media to tell us what to look at, and what not to look at. They herd us like sheep. It's kind of like the Church used to be. You know, the Church used to tell everyone what to believe. Well, the media's taken over that role. In the past, we were ruled by the Church and the State. Now it's the Media and the State.

MP: But who are *they*?

JG: Well, we don't know, do we? For obvious reasons, they keep their identities hidden. If we knew who they were, we'd most likely pitch them into the ocean. But we know they must be super-rich because money is power. So, it's a bunch of multi-billionaires. Many of them probably bankers.

MP: So, you think someone put the word out to make people think *Mars Attacks!* was bad?

JG: I do. I couldn't help noticing this haunted look in the faces of the executives. I mean, after the screenings, it was clear we had a hit on our hands, so why the long faces? But the executives knew something we didn't. My guess is some people from New York saw the previews and gave it the thumbs down. So, they released it, but spent little on the campaign and told the critics to pan it.

When I asked, I was told they spent ten million on the release. Then I was told twelve million. But I don't believe it. It had to be less than that. There was no evidence of a big campaign. The way they did it was the way they release independent movies. And a lot of my friends thought it was an independent movie. One of them called it: "The world's most expensive art movie."

Anyway, the bankers didn't have the same perception control in Europe – or not as much. So, even though the reviews were mostly bad, people went to see it, and word of mouth did the rest. Within days of its release, people were lining up to see it.

MP: Wow.

JG: It all comes down to money. People need money, and they want to be successful. And they've been made to believe that if they think for themselves they're gonna be poor. So, they need to find out what the word is, and follow it. And, if it turns out they're wrong, they have a good excuse: "Everyone else was doing it, so if you're going to fire me, you'll have to fire everyone else as well." It's safety in numbers. Film critics, especially, are vulnerable. They can easily be replaced. And they've got these cushy jobs. Imagine being paid to watch movies! I'd love that job!

MP: Me too! Ha ha! If I'd been paid for all the movies I've watched, I'd be rich!

JG: Yeah, so they don't want to buck the trend. They find out what the word is before they write their review. And they never stop to ask where the word is coming from.

MP: Where is it coming from?

JG: Well, I don't know. That's the problem. It really bugged me, this *Mars Attacks!* thing. I couldn't understand it! I kept asking people. I asked everybody. I mean, it was obvious something unusual was going on. All the guys on the film could feel it. But I think people were scared. They didn't want to talk about it.

And *Mars Attacks!* was a hit. It turned into a hit when it was released in Europe. And nine out of ten of all studio releases bomb. They lose money. Hits are rare and highly valued. And if you write or direct a hit, you're popular. Everybody wants you. Your phone never stops ringing.

But what happened to me after *Mars Attacks!* was the phone went dead. I couldn't get arrested. Before *Mars Attacks!* I was being offered writing assignments. After that, nothing. Not a dicky bird. And that was very strange. My phone should have been ringing off the hook.

And Tim was punished too. They screwed him around on *Superman Lives*, and then canceled it, and did other things too to make him suffer. Why? For what? For delivering a hit movie? It made no sense. I wanted to figure it out.

The audience reaction at the previews was ecstatic, so we should have been off to the races. But then this big blanket came down. One day, the executives were rubbing their hands in anticipation, and the next day, it was all over. The movie was a dud. Why? Someone had nixed it. I knew it wasn't Bob Daly or Terry Semel, the bosses of Warner Bros. They were both nice, regular guys who just wanted to do a good job and keep everybody happy.

Bob Daly told me he thought the movie was weird, but he kind of chuckled about it. He knew it would be popular, especially with the kids. And Terry Semel loved Tim. He was a fan of his work.

So, the only place it could have come from was head office. And head office is New York, Wall Street. The guys who bank-roll the studio. It had to be them.

MP: Okay, now, let's talk about some of the actors we haven't mentioned. And then we'll get on to the editing...

JG: All right. We didn't mention Sylvia Sidney, who played the old lady. She was wonderful. She was a big star back the 30's and 40's. I remember seeing her in *Sabotage*, a Hitchcock film, and falling in love with her. She was just so beautiful. And Tim cast her 'cause she was perfect for the part, and he adored her. She was in *Beetlejuice*, and he loved what she did in that. So, he wanted her, right from the outset. The old lady who saves the world. I didn't get to know her until I went to Kansas, when we were on location there, and we all stayed at the same hotel in Wichita.

MP: Was the Donut Shop there?

JG: Uh, no. I don't think so. That was done somewhere else. In California. But Kansas was weird. It's flat in all directions. Completely flat. It's eerie. 'Cause we're used to land going up and down, having a bit of ebb and flow to it.

One of the Kansas universities did a project called: "Is Kansas flatter than a pancake?" And what the students did was they used surveying equipment, like laser distance meters, to measure Kansas. I think it was about 300 miles across. And they calculated how flat it was. And it turned out it really was flatter than a pancake! Three hundred miles of completely flat land from one side of the state to the other.

MP: Wow!

JG: But, anyway, so we were in the hotel, and having breakfast, and I got chatting to Sylvia Sidney and, I mean, she was just fascinating. And we talked and talked, when she wasn't needed for her scenes, and she was full of stories. And, sometimes, she got very emotional. She was lovely. And it was so interesting hearing what it was like being a star at *Paramount* in the 1930's. The world was so different then.

We talked about everything. Her career, and her love life. She'd married three times. I asked her: "Which husband did you like the best?" And she said: "Lou Adler." I think he was her second husband. He was a very good actor who worked with the Group Theatre, run by Harold Clurman who was famous, along with Stella Adler, for introducing Stanislavsky's ideas about acting.

And Clifford Odets, who some consider one of America's best playwrights, wrote a play called *Golden Boy* for Harold Clurman, and Luther Adler played the Golden Boy, and won many awards, and was much admired.

Anyway, Sylvia married Luther Adler, and she loved him very much. She said he was absolutely the most wonderful guy, but she was doing films in L.A. and he was touring a lot. And, what happened was: he was unfaithful to her. And she was so angry at him for being unfaithful, and she had, she said, too much pride. You know, she was this movie star who everybody wanted to sleep with, but she was faithful to him. So, they fought and fought, and then she divorced him. He didn't want to get a divorce, but she wanted to punish him. And she said it was the biggest mistake of her life. She really, really regretted it.

Her view was that some men are alphas – alpha males. And that was the type she liked. Lou Adler was an alpha male. But, if you marry an alpha, you have to be realistic. You have to understand that he's going to have other women. But if you have a beta male, he'll be faithful to you. You can control him, and have a stable marriage, but it won't be as exciting as being married to an alpha. That was her view. And she said, after she divorced Lou Adler, she was never truly happy again.

MP: Oh…

JG: I wish I could remember all the stories she told about her days at Paramount. She said she was friends with Judy Garland. They shared a house together. This was before she was married to Luther Adler. Judy Garland was younger than her and at a different studio. MGM. And Judy was very fragile. The studio was giving her drugs to keep her working. And sometimes she would flush them down the toilet. But then she'd get depressed and refuse to work. So, B.P. Schulberg, who was running Paramount and was friends with the guys at MGM, asked her to look after Judy, and make sure she took her pills.

Sylvia said she grew very fond of Judy. And they both wanted to rebel against their studios, but were too young to know how. They both felt powerless. Sylvia Sidney was the girlfriend, the, um, secret girlfriend, of B.P. Schulberg, the head of the studio. B.P. Schulberg. He was married, with kids. She didn't like him. But she had to be his girlfriend. That's what she said. She said she was afraid of him. He was much older and very powerful. It was a kind of *droit de seigneur* thing.

These studio heads were like oriental potentates. Some of them had harems. Harems of starlets. But Sylvia wasn't a starlet. She was an A-list star, mainly because of B.P. Schulberg. That was the deal. He made her a movie star.

My guess is he was in love with her. I asked if her parents knew about this arrangement and she said yes, they knew about it. But, you see, it was the Depression, everybody was broke. Many people were starving. And Sylvia was a great beauty, as you can see in the pictures, and B.P. gave her these roles, and money. She had the best of everything. And she could help out her family.

I asked her about Alfred Hitchcock. "What was it like working with him?" She didn't like him. She said he was vulgar. And she wouldn't have anything to do with him. When she needed to say something to him, she'd do it through an assistant. She said he was a disgusting man and she refused to talk to him. Hahaha!

MP: Wow...

JG: And I said: "What was it like going to England to make *Sabotage*?" And, she said it was wonderful. Very exciting. She was in her early twenties, and she sailed over on the Queen Elizabeth, and she was given the top cabin, sort of the Royal Suite, and she was treated like a queen. And when she got to England, she was taken to some luxurious apartment in Mayfair, and she noticed that her sheets and pillowcases had the Royal crest on them. From the Royal Family. And she asked one of her assistants: "Why do the pillowcases have the Royal crest on them?" And she was told that the king – that would have been King George V – had been told she was coming, and ordered that the Royal sheets and pillows should be given to her for her personal use. See? That's how she was treated. Isn't it amazing? So, it's not surprising she had a bit of an ego!

And she was invited to Buckingham Palace, and she met the Royal Family, and had dinner with them. But Hitchcock didn't come up to her standards. He was too common! But he did a good job with *Sabotage* – and she's stunning in it. And she had a lovely way of underplaying, which was very modern.

Tim Burton at Caesar's Palace. Vegas.

Tim on his way to a meeting at Warner Bros.

Martians, JG + Jeff Field, agent.

Poppy in Ojai.

Ojai building.

JG + Lisa-Marie in Las Vegas.

Olga, JG and Lisa-Marie.

Virgil's House in the fall.

Emma Makinen.

JG and Tim - new T-shirts.

Wanna buy a script?

Whitley Heights.

The BeatNicks

The BeatNicks.

Glenn Shadix.

Fred Molina - Still from 'The Treat'.

Shaun Calley and Jacqui de la Fontaine.

Jonathan
Love you
mean it!
always
Lisa Marie

Lisa-Marie loves JG - maybe.

The incomparable Tim Burton.

She was a very good actress. Very talented. Most movie stars in the 30's, were stagey. Overdoing it. She was more real. The only other one like her was Louise Brooks.

So, yeah, we had a lot of conversations about lots of things... She did *Sabotage* the same year Judy Garland did *The Wizard of Oz*, which was in 1935. They were both contract players, working very hard and, when they weren't doing a film, they were having riding lessons, singing lessons, dance lessons, all kinds of things. They were constantly being trained. And, to get the most out of them, the studio would have them do five or six films a year. They'd finish one movie, have the weekend off, and start the next movie.

MP: Well, that was a good training, huh?

JG: Well, yes it was. It was intense. And some people said it was brutal. But when you look at those Chinese dancers, their training, it's much worse! Ha ha! And there is something to be said... I mean, the Bolshoi Ballet – the training they had – that was brutal too...

MP: And they produced really great performers. It seems to me, from what you were just saying, it would make the actor feel more secure – all that training. Whereas now they're kind of left. Are they kind of left on their own?

JG: Yes, they are.

MP: I imagine it would give you confidence, 'cause you're really part of the whole organization, and you have all these lessons; you have a schedule, even though it's difficult and challenging. And you feel like you are part of a team.

JG: Very true. They liked it. And people were very happy when they got a contract. 'Cause they had security for seven years. And lots of movie roles, usually. And they had friends. It's a bit like being at school. Though, at the same time, you weren't free. You couldn't leave Los Angeles. Not without permission. And you might hear they're making a movie at another studio, and there's a nice part for you in it, but you can't go up for it because you're under contract. There were a lot of restrictions. It's a balance. It's always a balance. Freedom and security.

MP: And, with all that training, if they stopped being a movie star, they would have these skills, like dancing, riding, or whatever...

JG: Hmm. Well, what I can say is: most actors were very upset when their contracts came to an end, or weren't renewed. This went on right up until the 1950's. Marilyn Monroe was gutted when she was dropped. She had a provisional contract with Paramount, I think, and she was expecting it to be renewed, but she was dropped. So, she was terrified. But, luckily, she got picked up by another studio.

But what Sylvia told me about Judy Garland was she was being pushed too hard. Overused. All those movies with Mickey Rooney. They were very popular and made a lot of money, so, they churned them out. And there was the whole sexual side of things. Sylvia didn't go into that too much, but she hinted that Judy Garland, and all the other young girls, were being passed around.

I got the impression that Sylvia was still bruised from her relationship with B.P. Schulberg. They parted on bad terms. She eventually rebelled against him, and they had fights, and then, when her contract came up, it wasn't renewed. So, she became a free agent. And I asked her, did she regret doing that? She said: "No." Even though she could have gone on for another seven years doing leads in big pictures, it wasn't worth it.

MP: But she probably had a lot of money saved, so that she could set herself up away from it all?

JG: Yeah, I think so. She went to New York and did theater. I asked her about other actors too. Other actors she'd worked with. One of her favorites was Herbert Marshall. She said he was a sweetheart. She didn't like Claudette Colbert though. Said she was a bitch! She knew everybody: James Cagney, Myrna Loy, Tyrone Power, Rudy Vallee, Joan Fontaine, Cary Grant. And she knew all the moguls: Darryl Zanuck, Irving Thalberg, Jesse Lasky, Harry Cohn – all those guys. She knew Preston Sturges, my hero. That was exciting, hearing about him. And she worked with Fritz Lang in a movie called *Fury*. "Fritz was an angel," she said.

So that was Sylvia. She was great. I took her out to dinner, and wished she was young again and we were out on a date. I asked if she'd be willing for me to interview her, and do a book about her life. She'd met all the U.S. presidents, and lived through the Depression and the Second World War... an amazing life. But she was a little reluctant, at first. She was a flirt, giving me the old 'maybe, maybe not.' Even though she was eighty or whatever, she would tease me. She said: "Well, I might let you do it, but you're gonna have to come visit me in New York, and I'll only consider it if you go to Brooks Brothers and buy a decent suit." You know, like that? And I wanted to do it. But the trouble was I was too busy.

MP: Is she still alive?

JG: No, she died. Such a shame. It was too soon! I wish I'd done that book. I mean, I was planning to send her flowers, and go to New York, and be charming, and prepare lots of questions. I would have loved that. I admired her so much. She was so sexy and feminine but also so *tough*. God! Those people from that generation, they went through such a lot, and they were hard as nails. Like Kirk Douglas, who just died, aged 103. They were superior to us in so many ways. We're so soft and gutless. That generation. Incredible people. I would have dearly loved to have spent a week in Manhattan interviewing Sylvia. I loved her company. And there was so much I wanted to understand. She was a fount of wisdom and experience. But I didn't have the time.

Halfway through the shoot, Sylvia Sidney was hit by a car while crossing the street in Manhattan. Everyone was really worried about her. But they weren't too surprised. You could just imagine her walking into the street and expecting all the traffic to stop.

MP: Hahahaha!

JG: Hahaha! Tim flew to New York and visited her in hospital. But she was okay. Although, the next time we saw her, she was looking a little battered and bruised. But tough as shoe leather and chain-smoking as always. And she'd cough. Oh, my God, she had a terrible cough. Cough, cough, cough! And, this deep, gravelly, smoker's voice.

Somebody would say: "God, Sylvia, you really should give up smoking." And she'd go: "Never!" But, a few years later she died of lung cancer. They put her through chemotherapy, the poor darling. She was so wonderful. Such a treasure.

MP: I want to ask you about other people in the cast. How about Pam Grier? What was she like?

JG: Pam Grier?

MP: Yes.

JG: Well, she was larger than life. Big personality. Big presence. When she entered the room, you knew about it! She was beautiful, statuesque, and she spoke in a kind of regal way. You know how strong she is on screen? Well, she's even stronger in real life. Most actors look bigger on screen. She looks bigger in real life. If you have Pam Grier in your movie, you need a different aspect ratio.

MP: Aspect ratio? What's that?

JG: It's like Cinerama or Imax 3D. A different film format. Pam Grier was really something. She was playing the mother, Jim Brown's ex-wife, and she was great. Tim loved her. He loved her old movies, like *Coffy*, *Foxy Brown*, and *Scream Blacula Scream*. We watched them together. So, I knew he'd like me to write a part for her, so I did. And she was available, which was very lucky. He was excited when she agreed to be in the movie. It was very good of her to do it, as it wasn't a lead role. And she was magnificent. Like Danny DeVito, she turned a small role into a big one. I love seeing her in the film.

I remember talking to her, on a lunch-break, about the plight of the Native Americans, and minorities being persecuted and so on. She told us she was part Cherokee Indian, part black, and part Hispanic. Three minorities rolled into one! And she was fierce. I wish she'd do more talk shows. She'd be great on talk shows. She was passionate about the racist treatment of blacks in the justice system, just like Jim Brown. But she was even more passionate about the Native Americans, who were treated much worse. They had everything taken away from them. They were slaughtered, almost completely. So, there's a lot of pain and hurt in the Native Americans. And it was kind of interesting, having the great Jim Brown, a black activist and leader, and then there was her.

MP: I know you're very interested in this subject...

JG: Yeah, of course... She was fascinating. And she was fun to have in the movie too. She's more of a star personality than an actress. But she knows how to craft a performance. Pam Grier's star quality was like being run over by a truck!

One guy I should say more about because he totally saved our bacon many times, is Larry Franco. He was the producer. And he was also kind of a line producer as well.

MP: What's a line producer?

JG: Well, he's the guy running the production. The producer, usually, is the person who puts the movie together. Develops it, puts the package together, and gets the money. And that's what Tim did. So, he was the producer. He produced *Mars Attacks!*

But, when Warner's hit the green light, he needed someone to take over and run things, so he could focus on directing.

He knew Larry Franco, I can't remember where from. I seem to remember meeting him before he came on to *Mars Attacks!* Larry had produced a lot of John Carpenter's movies.

Larry Franco is very reassuring. He's a big, warm bear of a man, with a great sense of humor, who's unflappable, which was needed on *Mars Attacks!* because it was one crisis after another. Larry's a problem solver. Nothing is too difficult for him. And I never saw him lose his cool. Not once. Although he did take a deep breath once or twice.

So, he looked after the logistics of the filmmaking, and liaised with the studio. And that's a difficult job, you need particular skills for that. It's like being the general in an army where you're dealing with the troops, communications, supplies, locations, transport, and you do a lot of troubleshooting.

Larry's expertise was both as a producer and a line producer. He had the diplomatic and business skills of a producer, as well as the show-running skills of a line producer. We were blessed to have him. And that was down to Tim who's very perceptive about people's qualities.

Actually, that is indispensable to good directing. Because movies are made by a team of artists, craftsmen, and fixers like Larry Franco. It's a group effort. And Tim is a talent-spotter. He spotted Danny Elfman when he was in *Oingo Boingo* and asked Danny to do the score for *Pee-wee's Big Adventure.* He'd never composed film music before. And he saw qualities in Michael Keaton that even Michael Keaton didn't know he had. And he persuaded him to do *Beetlejuice,* which paid off brilliantly. And he did it again with *Batman.*

Nobody wanted Michael Keaton for Batman. They thought it was insane. Keaton was a thin, wiry comedy guy. Batman was a linebacker, with muscles and a chin. An action hero. Everybody said *Batman* would be a colossal bomb. But

Tim insisted on Michael Keaton, and then came up with the muscular body-suit. No one could see what Tim could see. And he picked Victoria Thomas to do the casting. And there's no one better. And Colleen Atwood – the same. And Chris Lebenzon, the editor.

By the way, one of the John Carpenter films Larry Franco produced was *They Live*. Have you seen that?

MP: What's it called?

JG: *They Live*.

MP: I don't think so.

JG: You must see it. It's a classic. It was low budget, made for about $2million, and wasn't released in the UK. But it came out on video. All the John Carpenter films are worth seeing, but I think that one, *They Live,* was his best script.

So, Larry Franco was a very good person to have on *Mars Attacks!* because he understood the movie, and was familiar with making movies under difficult circumstances. He was always in a good mood, always cracking jokes, never stressed out by anything, and he put everyone at their ease. And he handled all of this whole, huge, crazy circus and, thanks to him, we never had any major screw-ups. Apart from the puppets at the beginning. That was a big screw up, but it was Larry who fixed that one.

I remember when we went to Vegas, with a small crew, to shoot the demolition of the Landmark Hotel. This happened before the official first day of production.

The Landmark used to be Howard Hughes's hotel. Larry Franco had heard about the planned demolition, contacted the owners, negotiated, and got permission to film it. So, we went out there. That was a real hotel being blown up in the film, not a model. And there was a hitch with that because they had a problem with the dynamite or something, 'cause it was supposed to happen during the day but was delayed until dusk. That's why the Martians attacking Vegas had to happen at night, which turned out better, because you can see all the dazzling Las Vegas lights. A much better atmosphere. Often, these screw-ups are blessings in disguise.

But one thing I have to say is that because Larry was so busy running the show, we didn't have anyone watching our backs at the studio. On *Batman*, there were two producers, Peter Guber and John Peters, who were talking to the studio every day, protecting the filmmakers, and prepping every stage in the process. We did have a studio executive assigned to us, who could have helped, but he wasn't really on our team. I never even spoke to him. I think Tim spoke to him but, most of the time he was AWOL. I called him multiple times. I thought he should more involved because we needed someone to keep things sweet with the studio. But he wouldn't take my calls. Why not? It was very frustrating! And when you're making a movie, you don't know what's going on at the studio. And there's always politics going on, and you have to keep abreast of that, to make sure someone's not gonna stab you in the back, or cut your budget, and also to get the marketing guys fired up. We didn't have anyone to do that.

And it turned out there *was* a lot of politics going on, with two factions at Warner's fighting each other. One faction wanted *Mars Attacks!* to succeed. The other wanted it to fail.

MP: Uh, I wanted to ask you about the French president, Tom Jones, Lisa-Marie, Poppy, and Christina Applegate...

JG: Okay. The French president. That was Barbet Schroeder. The day before the first day of shooting, I got a call from Tim, and he was in a bit of a panic, because the first scene they had to shoot was the one with the French president, and they didn't have an actor for it. So, he called and said: "We've gotta get somebody for tomorrow!" And I remember going blank. I couldn't think of anybody. Then it came to me. Barbet Schroeder!

Now, Barbet Schroeder was a director – not an actor – and he was my neighbor. He lived in Whitley Heights, where I was living in Hollywood, on this little hill, and Barbet was a friend of Laurie Frank's, my previous landlady.

Soon after arriving in L.A., I rented a room in Laurie's house. Laurie Frank was a screenwriter and Barbet was her friend, and he was this incredible guy who'd produced Eric Rohmer movies in France – these beautiful, very low budget movies, like *Pauline at the Beach*, *The Green Ray*, and *Claire's Knee* – often using film students.

So, I suggested Barbet Schroeder, and Tim didn't know him but they were shooting the next day, and he had a hundred things to do. He said: "What's he like?" And I said: "Well, he's perfect. He's tall, he's got a touch of Charles De Gaulle about him, but better-looking. He's not an actor, but he's charismatic, and it's only a small part, so you don't really need an actor. And he looks right. He's French and he's a director. He directed *Barfly* with Mickey Rourke and Faye Dunaway." And Tim said: "But is he available?" And I said: "I'll call him and find out." So, I called Barbet: "Are you doing anything tomorrow?" He said: "That depends…" I said: "Do you wanna be in a movie, directed by Tim Burton, playing the French president?" And he thinks for a moment, and says: "Yes, I can do that."

MP: The French! Hahaha! "Yes, I can do that!"

JG: So, I said: "Great. I'll tell Tim you're coming in tomorrow." He said: "They will have to send a car for me." I said: "Yeah, yeah. You'll get everything." So, I called Tim back and said: "He'll do it. He just wants a car to pick him up."

MP: He didn't ask for any money or anything?

JG: No.

MP: That's great! So cool.

JG: So, Tim said: "He's gonna have to come in early for costume fittings. Does he mind coming at 6 a.m.?" So, I said: "Hold on, I'll call him again." So, I called Barbet and said: "Can you come in at 6 a.m., 'cause they have to find a costume for you and do your hair and make-up." And he said: "Six in the morning? No, that's impossible." So, I asked him: "What time could you come?" And he said: "Ugh! Well, I suppose ten in the morning, but I would prefer eleven…"

MP: Hahahaha!

JG: So, I had to negotiate with him, and he finally agreed to 9 a.m. So, I called Tim back and I said: "He'll come at nine o'clock in the morning." So, Tim said: "Oh, fuck. Well okay. Nine in the morning, I guess we can do it."

MP: Because it's the last minute?

JG: Yeah. They were up against it. So, he said: "Tell him yes."
So, I said: "Well, you should tell him. It would be better coming
from you." So, I gave him the number, and Tim called him
and persuaded him to come in at 6 a.m. Hahahaha!

MP: Hahahaha! Virgo!

JG: Um, I didn't go down for the first day of shooting, 'cause
I was doing something else. But I went down for the second
day, and Tim said: "Where were you yesterday? It was the
first day of shooting!" That's a big day. Everybody shows
up. It's like a thing.

MP: Is it like a party or something?

JG: In a way. Lots of people show up – executives, agents,
and people like that. It's a get-together to celebrate the start
of production. It's a tradition like the wrap party at the end.
    Anyway, I showed up on the second day, and Tim said:
"Oh, where were you yesterday?" I said: "I didn't wanna
bother you. You know, you don't need extra people clogging
things up." Which I think is true, actually. But he said: "You
should have seen Barbet Schroeder. We shot his scene and he
was great." So, Tim was happy about that.
    And Barbet was an interesting guy. He told me that when he
was making *Barfly*, with Mickey Rourke and Faye Dunaway, he
said it was very difficult to get it made. It's very, very hard to
get a film made and released. You've got basically six studios
and each one makes, roughly, ten or twelve films a year. So,
you've got sixty or seventy films a year from the studios. And
you don't need more than that because the studios pick up the
best independent films for distribution as well. You don't want

the marketplace too crowded. So, you have about a hundred new movies coming out each year. Two new movies a week.

And everybody wants to get in on the studio movies because they're the best. The best funded, the best publicized, the best distributed. There are thousands and thousands of people who want to do them. According to the census, there are 800,000 actors in Los Angeles county. Eight hundred thousand!

MP: Whoa!

JG: And you've got all the producers, writers, directors, and crew people. So, it's very competitive. And if you can't get to make a studio movie, you try to make an independent and hope one of the studios picks it up.

Okay, so there was this independent film company called *Cannon Films*. Run by two Israeli guys, Golan and Globus. I think, later on, it turned out they were money laundering. Um, that was the rumor anyway, because they kept funding films that weren't released...

So, Barbet Schroeder... He went to *Cannon* with a script by Charles Bukowski, based on his novel. And he'd gotten Mickey Rourke to agree to play the lead. But, even with Mickey Rourke, it was tough to get the film financed.

Mickey Rourke has had an up and down career. At that time, he was in a 'down' phase, so Barbet couldn't get a studio, so he went to Cannon, and the boss – Menahem Golan – he said yes if Barbet could get another star to play the female lead. And Barbet, who's a miracle-worker, went and got Faye Dunaway.

Faye Dunaway hadn't worked in a while, but she was still a major star. Barbet, he's French, well, actually, Swiss-French, and he wooed her, and he's very charming, and it worked. She agreed to do it. And, oh God, she was brilliant in the film! She was amazing. People consider it one of her best performances. And Mickey Rourke was great too.*

And, so, Barbet showed up, and he said: "Good news Menahem! We've got Faye Dunaway! We can make the movie!" So, Menahem said: "Wow, you've got Faye Dunaway, really? You've really got her? You're not jerking me around?" So, Barbet said: "No, no. She's doing the movie." And he showed him her Letter of Intent, signed by her, saying she'd do it. So, Menahem said: "Well, I suppose we should do it then. What's the budget?" It was about two and half million, which was very cheap for a movie with two stars. So, he said: "Well, I suppose... I mean, we should do it then. Okay."

So, Barbet told Mickey and Faye Dunaway, and began to gather together his troops. Then, he goes back to Menahem Golan and says: "Okay, we need to make contracts with the stars, and money to start pre-production." And Menahem Golan says: "Nah, I've changed my mind. We're not gonna do it. I ain't got the money." And Barbet said: "But, you made a promise! I've told the actors. You have to do it!" He said: "No, no, I haven't got the money." And Barbet was: "But you have to do it!"

MP: Hahahaha! Yes!

JG: "Menahem, you must keep your word. You're a man of honor!" And Menahem said: "Well, yeah, but I haven't got the money. Would you mind leaving now, please?" "But you

---

* Bukowski said of his performance: "Mickey appeared to really love his role, and yet without exaggeration he added his own flavor, his zest, his madness, his gamble... without destroying the intent or the meaning of the character... I was very pleased with the love and understanding he lent to the role of the Barfly."

have to do this! What kind of a shit man are you?" Menahem says: "I don't care what you say! Fuck off!" So, Barbet left, and he was furious! He was absolutely furious. And he was having fantasies. He started having fantasies...

MP: Hahahaha!

JG: He said: "I am going to kill him! I'm going to get a gun from my street friends and go into his office, and I am going to shoot him!"

MP: Hahahaha! I love him! Hahahaha!

JG: And then he came up with a plan. He hired a registered nurse. And she had a nice uniform, a white uniform with a little hat, and she was a real nurse.

MP: Yes?

JG: And she had her identity card, to prove she was a registered nurse. And then he bought a small guillotine – like the ones they use for chopping the heads off cigars. He got one of those. And he went to the offices of *Cannon*. And he said: "It's me, Barbet Schroeder. I want to see Menahem!" And the receptionist, the secretary, got on the intercom, and she said: "No, he's not gonna see you. He's busy." And he said: "We're gonna wait here. And this is..." He introduced the nurse. "This is Shirley. She's a registered nurse. And this is a guillotine. And this is my finger. I'm going to put my finger in the guillotine and I'm going to cut it off unless I see Menahem. And the registered nurse is here to attend to my wounds."

MP: Hahahaha! The French!

JG: "You tell him I will wait for one hour, and if he doesn't open the door and see me, I will cut off my finger."

So, she got on the intercom and said to Menahem Golan: "Look, he's gonna cut off his finger. And I think he's serious." And Menahem said: "Tell him to go fuck himself!"

So, the secretary says: "Menahem Golan says could you please leave?" So, Barbet said: "I'll give him fifty-five minutes, and then the finger comes off. There will be a lot of blood. Please do tell him that." So, she gets Menahem on the intercom again and says: "Mr. Golan. He's really going to do it. He's going to cut off his finger if you don't see him." "I don't care! Let him cut his finger off!" And, so then they waited in the outer office, and then, five minutes before the deadline, Barbet said: "Call him again. We only have five minutes left." So, the secretary called him, but Menahem wouldn't come out of his office. Then, when there was just one minute left, the secretary called him again and, this time, he opened the door.

MP: Oh! Phew!

JG: And he looked at Barbet with his finger in the guillotine, and the registered nurse in her white uniform, with her medical box.

MP: My God!

JG: And when he saw this, and the expression on Barbet's face, well, he knew he was serious. And he freaked out. "No, no! Don't do it! Don't do it!" And he said: "All right, come in, come in." And Barbet got the money.

MP: Hahahaha! For the movie?

JG: Yeah.

MP: Hahahaha! Bravo! Wow!! (*Clapping loudly*)

JG: Hahaha! And they made a beautiful film. I mean it's one of the nicest films you could possibly see.

MP: Don't you love the French? Hahahaha! So dramatic! But he was serious!

JG: You bet. He's crazy. I visited him. Let's see, he moved out of Whitley Heights, and got a place in Venice, not too far from Venice Beach. But it was in the black area. An area controlled by the Crips, a street gang. And that's another story. I went to visit him there a couple of times, and it was a little intimidating. Because you've got Venice, right? The boardwalk, the beach, the canal area, and then, about four streets in, you cross over into Crips territory. It's all black. No whites at all. There were two major gangs in L.A., the Bloods and the Crips. And this part of Venice was controlled by the Crips.

MP: Oh, my God! I just saw online, he made a movie about a Buddhist monk! *Le Venerable W...*

JG: Did he? Oh, I didn't know that. He's a very good director. There was some criticism of him for selling out, 'cause he did some cookie-cutter movies, for money. But you've gotta make money somehow. (*Looking at a photo of him directing Le Venerable W*) Oh yeah, that's him. Yeah. He's very tall, and lordly. Long legs. Sort of looks like an eagle. And very charming. Laurie Frank, and all her girlfriends, were in love with him. Um, very eccentric.

So, what happened was this: I went down to his house, okay? And, nobody visited him there because it was so dangerous. And when I asked him: "Why do you live here?" He said: "Because it's so cheap."

MP: Hahahaha!

JG: He got a house, a big house, for almost no rent, you see? And he was sharing it with another French guy, an old friend of his, who was even more crazy than he was. And the reason I went down there was because Suzanne – Suzanne Fenn, the editor – who was a friend of his, told me he had an old car he wanted to give away. He didn't want to sell it for scrap, because he was fond of it. He wanted to give it away. Well, I needed a car, so I went down to look at it.

It was an old Chevy Nova. The ugliest car you've ever seen. And really beat up. But it had a V8 engine. And I knew this Greek Cypriot guy who had a machine shop. He'd been in the army, in the army transport corps. And he was great at getting vehicles to run. And, between us, we created a whole new chassis for it, using junk steel and scrap doors and suchlike. Anyway, I'm getting ahead of myself.

Uh… Let's see, I called him, first of all, to tell him I was coming over. I had a rental. I was in a rental car. And I asked him if I could come over, and he said yeah, and he said: "Don't park outside the house. They'll take the wheels."

MP: Hahahaha!

JG: He said: "There's a place you can park a couple of blocks away." There was a restaurant, and they had a parking lot. He said: "Park there, then walk the two blocks." So, that's what I did. I walked. And when I got to his house, it looked like it was in a war zone. The front door, and all the windows were covered in thick corrugated iron. So, I got there, right? And I knocked on the door. They had a peep hole. "Who is it?"

"It's me, Jonny."

"Okay."

So, I go in. And the place was very messy inside. They had lots of furniture they'd found on the street, or in thrift stores. Different sofas and things. It looked like a squat.

MP: Hahahaha!

JG: And um, but the house was big. It had a front porch, and it was big. Big rooms, and a big garden out back where they were growing vegetables and raising chickens.

MP: Hahahaha!

JG: Haha! And he was very proud of this place. He was saying: "It's great here. We have eggs every morning. Fresh eggs! It's wonderful! It costs us nothing!"

MP: Hahahaha!

JG: But I said: "Do you have any trouble with the Crips?" And he said: "Well yes, we do. We had to seal up the windows with steel sheets and corrugated iron, 'cause they were shooting at us through the windows."

MP: Jesus!

JG: And he said, when they first arrived, they took all the wheels from his car. And Barbet said: "I'm not having this! They can't take the wheels off my car! How do I get to work?" So, he went out, and he was knocking on doors, and asking everybody: "Who took my wheels?"

MP: Hahahaha!

JG: Hahahaha! He was saying: "I wanna know who did this!" And the black guys were like: "Who is this freak? What's wrong with him? Doesn't he know he's gonna get shot?!"

MP: Hahaha!

JG: And they've all got guns. But nobody shot him. They were kind of amazed by him. Like I said, he's got this presence. Like a duke or something.

MP: It probably helped that he was French.

JG: Yeah, it did. But it was his attitude. He was fearless, and he was scolding them. "Look, I want my wheels. I've gotta get to work!" And he paid one of the kids to find out who took them, and he went to where they were at and demanded them back. And they said: "How much? How much you gonna pay?"

MP: Hahahaha!

JG: Yeah! And they made a deal for like fifty bucks or something. And then Barbet told them to screw the wheels back on. And they said: "You are fucking kidding!"

MP: Hahahaha!

JG: You know: "You're lucky you're still in one piece!"

MP: Hahahaha!

JG: And he said: "Look, we've made a deal. We are men. We are men of honor..." He did all that, and he persuaded them! And they put the wheels back on for him.

MP: Wow, he's like a real president. Hahaha!

JG: And, yeah. He became friends with them, not all of them, but most of them.

MP: Wow, he must have had, kind of, protection like: "If you touch this man..."

JG: Yeah, I think he did. They allowed him to live there. He got a special dispensation. Because their policy was 'No Whites.' That's why they were shooting up the house, but Barbet said that he'd signed the contract for the house, so he wasn't gonna leave. But they still used to raid his chickens. They climbed over the wall to steal the eggs, and they tried to take the chickens as well.

MP: Hahaha!

JG: And they had a couple of fights over that.

MP: So, he loves drama?

JG: Certainly! There was always a drama going on with him. So, he gave me his car. The Chevy Nova. And me and Nikos fixed it up. It had a lot wrong with it. But when you have a wreck with a good engine, you can customize it. We put a new stainless-steel grill on it. Looked like shark's teeth. And I had the whole car sprayed silver. It looked like a silver shark. And it was a good car. I drove to Vegas in it many times, and to Ojai, and El Paso, in Texas. That was a long drive, through Arizona and New Mexico. And it was very roomy. Bank seats. You could sit three in the front.

And then, one day, I was visiting Laurie Frank and the car was parked outside her house. And Barbet Schroeder was there. And we were chatting and he saw the car out the window. And he went: "Look at that! I've never seen a car like this. Whose car is that?"

And I said: "It's my car."

"*Your* car?"

I said: "Yeah. It's your car actually. It's the one you gave me. I changed it."

"You mean this is the Chevy Nova? But it looks completely different!"

I said: "I gave it a makeover."

"But this is amazing! I've never seen such a car. I want it back!"

MP: Hahahaha!

JG: He made me give it back. I had to give it back to him.

MP: Hahahaha! You know these Hollywood guys, they must have thought: "These weird Europeans. The Englishman and the Frenchman..."

JG: Well, I don't know. But I didn't wanna give it back.

MP: Did he pay you for the work you did on it?

JG: No. Hahaha! He didn't. Later on, Barbet became very successful. He directed some Hollywood films, like *Single White Female* and *Reversal of Fortune*, with Jeremy Irons, and some others, and he became an A-list Hollywood director. He did very well.

My other memory of Barbet was Laurie's dog. A boxer, a female boxer, that was Laurie Frank's dog. The dog loved Barbet. Her name was Mega. And, in L.A. the dogs are just as bizarre as the people. Sometimes, to help Laurie, I took Mega for walks. To give her some exercise. I used to take her to the Errol Flynn Estate, which was an area of wilderness in the middle of Hollywood. There was a dispute over who owned the estate, so it was like no one owned it, and people used it for jogging, and walking their dogs. And Mega was a sweet dog, but she was eccentric. She would attack black people, and people on bicycles, and old ladies with packages.

MP: Oh, my God!

JG: The reason I mention the dog is because Barbet, when he came over to Laurie's place, he had this habit of... Um, he would sit on the sofa, with the dog on his lap, and masturbate her.

MP: No!

JG: Yeah! While we were sitting there, having coffee.

MP: What? In front of everyone?

JG: Yeah. She loved it. She was in heaven.

MP: Jesus!

JG: That's probably why she got so excited every time he showed up.

MP: Hahahaha! Oh, my God!

JG: So, anyhow, he did a good job on *Mars Attacks!* Tim told me he did his scene in three takes. So, what's next?

MP: How was Lisa-Marie on the film?

JG: She was great. She was as good as anyone else, which I think proved my point that she was A-list material. And she was sweet.

During pre-production, it used to touch my heart how dedicated she was. She did everything she could to prepare for the role. Acting class, gym, pilates, yoga, and studying the script and thinking hard about different approaches to the character. She really, really wanted to be a movie actress, and was hell bent on doing everything she could to achieve that. And she was always early, always prepared. And that spooky walk she did – she worked that out herself. She created that, and it was hard to do.

MP: I heard that her wig was so heavy, she still had the scar from it. Is that true?

JG: Yeah, that's right. She had a little scar at the top of her forehead. No, she was dedicated. She liked torturing herself for her art. And she was absolutely perfect as the Martian Girl. She should have had lots of parts. That's what she needed. She needed experience. She had the talent, the raw material. But she was an actress of a different stripe. She wasn't a theater actress. She was more like Johnny Depp. I think she could have become a real asset if she'd been given more parts. She had a good agent, so I never understood why that didn't happen.

I tried to cook up some things for her but, it was odd, there was always some kind of obstruction. It's so very hard to make it in Hollywood. Even if you're beautiful and talented. I thought she could be a star. Like a modern Janet Leigh. Did I tell you I introduced them, Tim and Lisa?

MP: Yeah.

JG: I think it was in... it must have been 1993. Me and Tim were in New York City. I remember it was New Year's Eve, and we wanted to do something. Go out. And I knew this girl, Olga Liriano, who was in fashion, and kind of a socialite. She introduced me to Andy Warhol one time, and she knew all these people. So, I called her up and I said: "Hey, what's happening?" My memory's a bit fuzzy but I think she said something about a party. Going to a New Year's Eve party. But I don't think we went. I think we went to a lap-dancing club instead. They were new at the time.

Anyway, she said... Olga said she had a girlfriend staying with her, and could she come too? So, I said: "Who is it?" And she said: "Her name's Lisa-Marie." And I said: "Is that the same Lisa-Marie who did *Something's Jumping in my Shirt* with Malcolm?" Because Malcolm McLaren had discovered Lisa-Marie when she was fourteen, and made an album with her. And Olga said: "Yes. Do you know her?" And I said: "Yes. Put her on." So, Lisa came to the phone and I asked her if she remembered me. And she said yes, she did. So, I made a plan with Olga to go somewhere, and Tim was happy about that, and he ordered up a limo. Because it was New Year's Eve, and Olga lived a long way uptown.

So, when we arrived in the limo, Tim waited in the car, and I went up to Olga's flat, which was on the fifth floor, and I met Lisa-Marie, who was now all grown up. The last time I'd seen her she'd been fifteen years old. Now, she was twenty-five and very beautiful. When she got into the car with us, Tim went quiet. Hahahaha!

MP: Did they get together that night?

JG: Oh no. They dated for a while. It took a while. She was working as a hat-check girl in a trendy restaurant downtown. Tim used to pick her up after work. She was lovely. A dream walking. And, later, she came up to a house I was renting in Upstate New York, from a friend of mine named Virgil Young. And I think it was there that Tim and Lisa-Marie got together.

But, on *Mars Attacks!* I barely saw her. I didn't see her shoot any of her scenes. If I wasn't needed on set, I didn't go. But I remember her being excited about it, and dedicated, like she was on *Ed Wood*.

MP: How did they do that, when she's taking off her head with a Martian head underneath?

JG: That was done in post. Post-production. Um, I don't know how they did it. It was very clever.

MP: And what about Poppy? How was she in the film?

JG: Not bad. Tim hired a dog-trainer. So, she did a lot of rehearsing! And the trainer brought another chihuahua, who looked almost exactly like Poppy, as an understudy. In some of the scenes it's the other dog, not Poppy, doing it.

MP: And Tom Jones. What was Tom Jones like?

JG: Okay, well, there's a story behind that… Originally, I'd thought it would be good to have a cheesy Las Vegas singer performing onstage when the Martians crash in. And, in the script, I wrote in Tom Jones as the singer. And then, one day, during pre-production, Tim called me and said Tom Jones was at, I think, Caesar's Palace. And, at that time, the agents were talking to Tom Jones about maybe doing a cameo in the film, and they thought it would be good if Tim said hello to him, as a courtesy. So, Tim said: "Let's go to Vegas and catch the show."

So, we flew to Vegas. Lisa-Marie came too. And we watched the show.

Now, I'd never seen him live before. And neither had Tim or Lisa-Marie. And he was really, really good. His voice was amazing! And he was buff. You could see he worked out a lot. He was a really impressive figure. Not cheesy at all. And, after the show, I said to Tim: "Man, he's really good!" And Tim said: "Yeah, he is. He's really good. He looks like an action hero." And we both had the same thought. That he should be a character in the movie. Not a cameo.

And so, after the show, we were shown into his green room – his reception room behind the stage – and there were people there, milling about. And there he was, Tom Jones, tall, buff, and radiating charisma. Well, we talked, and he was easy to talk to. And I was star struck. The person he most reminded me of was Sting. They have a similar presence. And they're both masters at working an audience.

So, after that, me and Tim discussed how to insert him into the story. So, I got to work on that, and concocted a through-line for him, which resulted in him ending the movie! It was inspirational, seeing Tom Jones in Vegas. And it gave us our ending.

And I remember laughing when I wrote the last scene, in Lake Tahoe, with Tom Jones surrounded by animals, and the music of *It's Not Unusual*. Because everything in the film, and the ending itself, with the animals and Tom Jones, is very unusual!

But the studio didn't like the new ending. They thought it was ridiculous. Which, of course, it is! They demanded I change it, and they were very serious about it. And the blood drained into my boots, because I really liked the ending. So, I spoke to Tim about it, and he said: "Nah, don't worry about it. Keep the ending."

MP: Wow, that's great!

JG: Yeah. Tim was wonderful. And I loved watching him work. Like the Martian Girl's dress. He went through a whole lot of designs before he got to the one you see in the movie. And when it came to making and fitting the dress, Lisa-Marie had to be sewn into it!

And the spaceships. The Art Department was top-notch, and they came up with lots of good drawings of different spaceships. But Tim didn't like any of the designs. So, he spent a lot of time drawing and finally getting the gloriously naïve flying saucers you see in the movie.

Tim designed pretty much everything you see in the movie. He said to me once he'd rather be a production designer than a director. That's what he liked the most. He's a visual artist and designing movies is fantastic for a visual artist. Because you're designing everything – clothes, interiors, and every frame of the movie is a picture. Tim would draw the whole movie. Visualize everything. That's what makes him so special, I think. His visual inventiveness, and his visual taste. And, to tell you the truth, he always had a bit of a problem with the production designers on his films, hahahaha!

MP: Hahaha! Yeah, I guess because he's a production designer himself.

JG: Yeah. I sometimes got the feeling he was jealous of Wynn Thomas, the production designer on *Mars Attacks!*

MP: Now, I don't wanna forget to ask you this. I know we were talking a bit about the Martians and the animation part, but I wanted to know about the *Ak! Ak! Ak!* sound of the Martians because people are saying it was a duck sound. Is that what it is – a quacking duck?

JG: That's close, but it's not that, no. See, when I was writing the script, I was living in Whitley Heights in Hollywood. I was sharing a house with this very clever and beautiful French film editor named Suzanne Fenn. She'd edited lots of movies; I can't remember them all. *Pretty Baby* was one, and *Dancehall Queen*.

And I had a little deck outside, a wooden deck. With trees and vegetation all around it. And there were these two birds. A pair of blue jays. And I was feeding them peanuts. I put the peanuts on the windowsill, and they'd swoop down and eat the peanuts. And they made this really unpleasant, ear-piercing staccato sound that kind of drilled into your head. And it was such a nasty sound, it kind of amused me because birds are supposed to sing, not squawk in this horrible way. I mean, you would never want to have a blue-jay as a pet! They sat in the trees, and when they saw me come in, they'd go: *Ak! Ak! Ak! Ak!* They were like these evil birds sent by Satan to torment me! So, when I was thinking about how the Martians talked, I thought they would talk like that. Hahahaha!

MP: Hahahaha! Oh, I've got a note here. It's from when you were talking about Jim Brown, and the plantation system he was telling you about. And then you jumped into something else. What is the plantation system?

JG: Well, it was the system they used on the plantations for governing the slaves. Jim Brown had researched it all. It was based on Roman slave manuals. And, basically it was 'divide and rule.' The problem for the slave-owner was: 'What if the slaves rebelled?' Well, he'd be wiped out, wouldn't he? And this is what happened in Haiti, where the slaves rebelled, and killed the plantations owners, and took over the island.

So, the answer was to divide the slaves into different groups, different factions, and this was done by setting the house slaves against the field slaves, by inciting envy in the field slaves by giving privileges to the house slaves. Then the field slaves were divided by giving the older men more privileges than the younger men.

Um, and there were tricks like giving white dolls to the kids. Giving them the idea that white was good and black was bad. And slaves with light skins got more privileges than slaves with dark skins. So, the women became more attracted to light-skinned men because they had more privileges, and that caused lots of hostility between the dark-skinned and the light-skinned men.

The light-skinned women would often be taken off the fields and become house slaves. So, the black girls thought they were uglier than the mulatto girls. The master was able to control hundreds of slaves that way because their resentment was directed at other slaves. Not at him. And if, from time to time, a slave disobeyed orders, or broke the laws, they had a system for dealing with that too. It was originated by a plantation owner named Lynch who wrote a book on slave management.

Lynch maintained that, to keep things stable, the master had to be seen as... he had to appear to be benevolent. A benevolent father who loved his children. So, the master should rarely, if ever, punish the slaves. This was done by a magistrate from another district, who would come in and they would have a court case and then the rebellious slave would be hanged from a tree in a public place, as a warning to the others.

MP: Is that where lynching comes from?

JG: Yes, it is, that's right. And the magistrate was blamed, you see? Not the master. That was the idea. And sometimes the master would beg for leniency. So, the slaves would think he was a nice bloke. And, at Christmas, the master would give presents. He was like Father Christmas. He'd give them presents. And at Easter time he'd put on a banquet for them. And he'd also have sex with a lot of the slave girls who would then have his children. And most of the women liked to do that because it meant that their children, their half-caste children, would have a better future. And it also produced a kind of, of loyalty between the women and the master. The masters didn't only do it 'cause they were horny. It was political. They were creating a kind of class system. And that's what class systems are – a way for a small élite to control large numbers of people. So, yeah, this is what Jim Brown explained to us.

MP: Wow...

JG: And it was a revelation to me because, when I thought about it, I realized that's pretty much how things are now in jolly old England! Hahaha!

MP: Wow. Well, thank you Jim Brown, for sharing it. Did he say anything about the script?

JG: No. Not to me.

MP: He was fantastic in it! I love him. He's got this big-hearted, open face.

JG: Yeah, he was perfect. I liked his character. A big strong, wounded guy. And kind of ludicrous.

MP: Uhuh? So, then that takes me to Christina Applegate. She was good.

JG: Yes, she was. A wonderful actress, and brilliant at comedy. We were so lucky to have her in that role. We had a great cast, didn't we?

MP: Yeah!

JG: Her facility for acting was impressive. She was like Michael J. Fox in that way. She had a similar 'acting machine' quality. She could just turn it on. Very professional. She'd been on a very popular TV series called *Married with Children* for a long time, and had learnt her craft extremely well. She was a delight. I wanted her for the lead role in *The Treat*, which I was directing. And she agreed to do it. Um, and, but I kind of mishandled it. *The Treat* told the stories of three prostitutes working in a brothel, which confused some people because they thought it was... They expected it to be, I don't know, soft-porn or something. Which I guess is understandable. But if you read the script, it's not like that. It's really a comedy about how stupid men are.

It was based on a play co-written with my mother, Pam Gems, which I put on, quite successfully, in London. There wasn't any sex in the film. Or nudity. It was about male fantasies. In that sense, it was kind of in the vein of movies like *The Seven Year Itch*, but more modern. Anyway, Christina pulled out because, she thought it was going to be salacious. I failed to convey to her how I was doing it. Or, maybe she didn't trust me. I'm not sure.

Anyway, she became nervous about it. I was very disappointed when she pulled out, but it wasn't the end of the world because we got Julie Delpy, and she was fine. Christina would have brought out more of the comedy, I think, but the emotional way Julie played it was very good.

MP: What about research? Did you do much research for *Mars Attacks*!?

JG: Yes, quite a bit. I didn't have to research Las Vegas because I knew it. Tim liked to go to Vegas for a break, to get out of L.A., so we went to Vegas a lot, so that's why I chose Vegas as one of the locations. And, then we had to have the Mid-West, and I picked Kansas, really at random. Because it was rural and a complete contrast to Vegas and New York. Later, I had to cut New York out for budget reasons. Uh, and I chose Washington D.C., because it made sense the Martians would attack the nation's capital, right? Plus, it was central to the theme. But I didn't know Kansas or Washington, so I did a lot of research and, when I told Tim I was planning a research trip to Washington D.C., he said: "Let's go together."

So, we went there. Tim, me, and Lisa-Marie. And it was great because Tim got the Warner Jet. Warner Bros had a private jet, which was very hard to get the use of. But Tim put in a request and they told him: "Oh, the Warner Jet is available at such and such a date." And then he asked the studio to get in touch with the White House and they did, and they arranged for us to have a private tour of the White House and maybe meet Bill Clinton, who was the president.

MP: Did you meet the president?

JG: Well, let me tell you what happened. We got on the Warner Jet, okay? And we flew to Washington in luxury. And Poppy was with us, the chihuahua, and we went to the White House and had this private tour.

A woman with neat hair, an Arkansas accent, and a ramrod-straight back took us through the rooms. And she talked like: "And this is the Blue Room, and this is the Madison Room. This is the East Wing." And we went all around, which was very useful.

MP: And were you writing it down?

JG: Yeah, yeah, yeah! I was writing everything down. And I was looking at the portraits and everything. And all that's in the movie. There's one bit where the Tour Guide – 'cause I used the Tour Guide based on *our* tour guide – in the scene with the school kids, and she says: "This is a portrait of James Monroe," which is what our tour guide said to us: "This is a portrait of James Monroe."

Um, so it's always very useful doing this kind of research, but then I may have put my foot in it. You see, I'd met this production designer named Ken Adam who had designed the early James Bond films. He was an amazing designer. And he did *Dr. Strangelove*. I had dinner with him with a fabulous man called Sandy Lieberson who'd been the president of Fox Studios at one time. He'd moved to England and married an English girl called Sarah Parkin, and he was producing films in London. Sandy Lieberson.

And we had dinner at his house, and we talked about *Dr. Strangelove* and he said someone had told him Richard Nixon, when he became president, asked to see the War Room. And the people at the White House were a bit surprised because there *wasn't* a War Room. So, Nixon had one put it. And, apparently, it looks like Ken Adam's set from *Dr. Strangelove*.

So, there we were in the White House and I was curious to know if this story was true. So, I asked the tour guide: "Is there a War Room under the White House?" And she went very quiet, and started fiddling with her hands. Then she asked us to look after ourselves for ten minutes. And she disappeared, and when she came back, we carried on with the tour.

Now, at the end of the tour, we were supposed to go to the Oval Office to meet Bill Clinton, but the tour guide said: "Oh, change of plan. Bill's been called away, so we won't be going to the Oval Office now." Naturally, we were a bit disappointed.

And I couldn't help wondering if it might have been because of my question about the War Room. Maybe it was classified? But it probably wasn't. That's just my fantasy. Anyway, we had a good time in Washington. Being with Tim is always fun, because he looks at everything in a humorous way.

It's like, we'd be looking at the Washington Monument and he'd make a joke about it. Because it's very phallic. Washington has a weird vibe. It was laid out by Freemasons and it's full of cabbalistic monuments and symbols. It's impressive, but it's also spooky and sinister. It makes you think of sadomasochistic sex parties...

But it was a valuable trip and, as I said, scripts evolve. You see, whenever you bring in something, you have to think about what to say about it. So, for example, if you bring in the military, you have to ask yourself: "What do I think about the military?" And, I personally, I have to say, that I think it's brainwashing. I mean, when I was... I went to a boarding school called Stowe School, in Buckinghamshire. And every Wednesday afternoon, we did army training. Wednesday afternoon. We were taught unarmed combat, how to use a knife and a garrotte, how to shoot rifles. How to kill people, basically. And we had to wear uniforms, and march, and do parades, and run through an obstacle course with a heavy pack, and all that stuff. And we played war games.

If you want to know what that was like, watch the movie *If...*, by Lindsay Anderson. He portrayed it perfectly. And so, we were trained to obey. To take orders. Don't think. Obey. Don't think. Obey.

MP: So, that's Jack Black?

JG: Exactly. When he's disassembling, and reassembling his rifle with a blindfold, he's drilling himself, and his Dad is proud of him. He's timing him. Jack Black is completely trained and brainwashed. And when the Martians come, he runs out to shoot them, and he's killed immediately. Hahaha! He's running into his own death. Because he's not thinking!

MP: Yes! He's following orders. He's given the responsibility of his life to other people.

JG: Right. And when he goes to fire his gun, the reality of the situation makes him so anxious, he makes a mistake. The point is that real life is different to training. And actually, what you need to do is learn how to think for yourself. Then you'll be a better fighter, and survive longer.

MP: Like the two black kids in the White House, who grab the Martians' weapons and use them against them.

JG: Exactly! So, when you write a script, this is what you do. You ask yourself: "What do I think about this?" If you're depicting the military, or anything else, it needs to be purposeful. So, if you're asked to write a film about Martians invading the earth, one thing you need to think about is: "What are people's attitudes to the invasion?" And, of course, people's attitudes are conditioned by their characters and by what's happening in their lives. So, with Annette Bening, for instance, she's trying to purify herself, to distance herself from her past and her bad deeds. She's running away from her trauma and depression by using the power of positive thinking and embracing New-Age values. Her mantra is: "Love and Peace."

And General Decker, who's seen carnage and death in wars, well, his attitude is different. So, all these things are developed out of logical thinking.

And when the Martians blow up the Capitol building, you ask yourself: "How does this affect people? How do they respond to this?" And, in that case, I wasn't sure how the residents of the nursing home would react. Would they be frightened? And then I thought, well, most of them will be on heavy medication, so they probably wouldn't react at all – which would be funny. But I wasn't so sure, so I went to Tim and we talked about it. And he liked that they were medicated zombies, but Sylvia Sidney was in that scene, and he didn't want her medicated because of all the other things she was doing in the film. Also, I believe Tim was visualizing Sylvia as his grandma, whom he loved, and who was a feisty, tough-old bird, who despised politicians. So, it was Tim who came up with the line: "Hurray! They blew up Congress!"

MP: I love that line! Hahaha!

JG: Yeah, and not long after that, I learned that Congress only had an 8% approval rating. So, most Americans feel the exact same way!

MP: That was so funny. Oh, my God! Hahaha!

JG: They call Washington D.C. "The District of Criminals."

MP: Hahaha. Yeah.

JG: And then you've got your characters. You have to know who your characters are. The easiest way to do this is to base them on people you know. But, sometimes, you can't do that, so you might base them on people you've read about, or seen on TV.

I had a big problem with the U.S. president. I didn't know who he was, and I didn't fancy any of the recent presidents because they'd be too recognizable and there was no value in satirizing them because they'd all been done on *Saturday Night Live*. And we were bored with them. Although I did, for a while, think he might be a bit like Ronald Reagan. I remember sketching out a scene where the President and First Lady see an astrologer.

MP: An astrologer?

JG: Yeah. About the Martians.

MP: Did Ronald Reagan consult astrologers?

JG: Sure. Him and Nancy were really into it. They never made a move without consulting an astrologer first.

MP: That's smart! I didn't know that. Hahahaha!

JG: Yeah, but I wasn't excited by doing a version of Ronald Reagan, so I was stuck. I was really stuck! You know: who is the president? *Who is he?*

MP: Did you want a likable character, or what?

JG: I didn't know! I was really stuck and he was an important character, so I was getting desperate. I couldn't get anything from freewheeling my mind, so I approached the problem logically.

MP: Logically?

JG: Yeah, from the ground up. You start with: "What is a leader?" Well, a leader is someone who leads. What are the chief characteristics of a leader? And that made me think of a book I'd read by a man called Michael Chance. In the book, his idea was that there are two kinds of leaders. He called them *agonic* and *hedonic*. Agonic – that is tough, aggressive. He got this from studying monkeys. Monkeys and apes. Some monkeys, like baboons, are agonic. They're aggressive. If a leopard threatens the troop, the baboon will fight the leopard, and probably get killed. But while he's fighting, the rest of the troop gets away. He saves the other baboons at the cost of his own life. That's agonic. Agonic leadership. That's like the warrior kings of old, and dictators such as Lenin, Stalin, Mao, and Pol Pot. They use force and aggression.

Then you have the hedonic type, and they rule through display. The chimpanzee is an example. When the leopard threatens the chimp troop, the leader will dance, or make funny noises. It will entertain and distract the leopard, so the other chimps can run away.

MP: What about the leader chimp? Does he get eaten?

JG: Sometimes he can be, yes. But usually he confuses the leopard so much, he's able to escape. So, in countries that are democratic, or semi-democratic, the leaders are nearly always hedonic. The American presidents are. The last one who wasn't was General Eisenhower. Because presidential candidates need to entertain the public to get votes. So, that was my first step. The president had to be hedonic. An entertainer.

But I couldn't find a model. I didn't like Clinton. Reagan was quite good. And I thought about Ross Perot, which might have been funny. And there were some colorful politicians in the past, like Teddy Roosevelt and Huey Long. I looked into Huey Long, whose slogan was "Every man a king." And I kind of shuffled elements of these guys to concoct the president. He had to be someone you'd believe the people would have voted for. A charismatic guy who was a bit of an actor, but also an alpha male.

MP: That sounds like Jack Nicholson.

JG: Yes, it does. But here's the thing, I still needed more than that because, when you create a character you have to get inside his skin. Otherwise, you don't know how he's going to feel, or how he's going to think. And then there's the dialogue. You have to know how he talks. And I didn't have a lot of time to do this. So, I used Tim.

MP: Tim? What do you mean?

JG: Well, Tim's an alpha male and an entertainer, and I knew how he talked, so I based it on him,

MP: Wow! He's the president?

JG: Yeah. That might surprise some people because the president doesn't seem like Tim, but actually, yes, it was largely based on him.

MP: Does Tim know?

JG: No. I never told him. You see, Tim can be, especially when he's directing, quite presidential. And when you're directing a movie like *Batman* or *Batman Returns*, big movies like that, you're in that kind of position. You're like the president of this big team of people who are making the movie. It's a similar role.

MP: Right.

JG: When Tim directs, his body language changes. He stands up very straight. He looks taller. His neck gets longer and he kind of swivels his head around, and he marches about. And he's alert – looking at everything and listening to everybody. And he's warm. So, that's how I wrote the president. Like that. And then Jack added things. He added a quite a lot. He invented lots of nice details.

MP: And it was just absolutely brilliant. Hahaha! I'm just remembering that scene, when he's just about to shake the hand of the Martian. Hahaha! That's just crazy! The uncomfortable way he's looking down at the Martian. Hahaha!

JG: Hahahaha!

MP: It just catches you! You can't stop watching him!

JG: Yeah. No, it's true. He's very inventive. You know, it's a cliché, but they say the poet or the artist is close to madness. And it's true. I've seen it in Tim. I've seen him teeter on the edge of madness sometimes. And Jack's the same way.

MP: What about you? Hahahaha!

JG: Not me. I'm totally sane.

MP: Hahahaha!

JG: I've… I have done though. A few times. You go a bit nuts. If you're working a lot and you're in this imaginative realm, you're in another world, and you start to go a bit crazy.

MP: Hahaha! Yes.

JG: But wonderful things come out of it. You sort of let the demons out. You let the angels out. Um, you become a channel for the forces.

MP: It's almost like downloads.

JG: It can be like that, yes. Like you're a sort of medium. And I think actors have that particularly because they're doing it with their whole body, mind, and spirit, you see? So, they really do become possessed.

INTERVIEW 4

FEBRUARY 9TH 2020

MP: One element we haven't talked about is the visuals, the design, and the special effects.

JG: Right. Well, that all came out of Tim's head. The spaceships, the Martians, the ray-guns – the nuclear missile exploding and being inhaled by the Martian Commander like he's smoking a bong...

MP: Yeah. Hahahaha!

JG: The guys at Industrial Light & Magic and Warner Digital did a very good job. I met some of them, and they were nice guys, very enthusiastic and diligent. Very open. They loved a challenge. So, when Tim said he wanted Sarah Jessica Parker's head on Poppy's body...

MP: Hahahaha! Was that in the script?

JG: Sure. Of course. But that was Tim's idea to do that. D'you remember the robot? The big giant robot?

MP: Yeah, yeah!

JG: With the little Martian driving it? Chasing Lukas Haas down the road? Tim came up with that. And the stuff inside the Martian spaceship, when the Martians are taking guns off the walls, getting into their battle armor, and climbing into the robots. Tim created all that. All I'd written was: *MONTAGE: the Martians prepare for battle.*

MP: That's amazing, I love that!

JG: Yeah, you see, that's what he's brilliant at.

MP: Was that made by special effects?

JG: Yeah, graphics and CGI.

MP: What about the robes? The Martian Ambassador and the Martian Commander's robes?

JG: That was CGI designed by Tim. I remember him doing these detailed paintings of the Martians, and trying out different cloaks, different designs.

MP: Jesus Christ. It must have been tons of work!

JG: Yeah! Tim can sometimes come across like he's lazy. But he's not at all. He works like a demon. It's funny because when he's not working, he's the most relaxed guy in the world. But when he's on something, he's a totally different person.

MP: Is it like obsessively working when he's working and, when he's chilling, it's like obsessional chilling?

JG: Yeah. Hahahaha!

MP: Hahahaha! I can relate to that.

JG: Yeah, but, no it's great to work with a good artist. He's the best I've ever worked with. I mean, I haven't done that much, but I did about ten plays in the theater and, I mean, there were hardly any artists there…

MP: That leads me onto the question: what for you is a true artist? Because, obviously, at least in my opinion, there's a huge difference. When somebody is a real artist there's something otherworldly about them. What for you is a real artist?

JG: I think it means originality. Real artists are rare. Not many of 'em. They're like white peacocks. I've only met a few in my life. I remember… I'll give you an example… When I was fifteen, I started at a new school. A state school in London. And, I went in… I'd only been there a few weeks… I went into the classroom and there was about five or six kids, same age as me, at the back, and they were crowded around somebody.

I went up to see what they were doing, and it was this boy – and he was drawing cartoons really, really fast. The other kids were watching him. And, this boy was amazing! The other kids were saying: "Draw this teacher, draw that teacher!" They were giving him instructions, and he was drawing them.

MP: Wow…

JG: And you recognized them. He caught them: the history teacher, the French teacher… And his cartoons were really funny. Everybody was laughing.

MP: Their personality was there?

JG: Yeah! And I was a cartoonist myself. I used to do the same thing – amuse other kids by drawing cartoons. But he was better than I was. And, because of that, I got to know him, and I had an idea, mainly because of him, to do a comic. To publish a comic – so his drawings could be in the comic. I figured I could write stories and he could do the drawings. And, I did it. I started the comic and we published seven issues of it.

MP: What is it called?

JG: It was called *It's All Lies*. And he was in every issue. He composed most of his cartoons himself. I didn't do much of the writing, just bits, and suggestions and stuff. And he did the most wonderful work.

MP: Do you have the copies of that?

JG: I do somewhere.

MP: I would love to look at them.

JG: His name was Matthew Freeth, and he was an artist.

MP: Where is he now?

JG: He lives in L.A. He does animation for Disney. Yeah, I saw him over there.

MP: So, it's interesting to me how you... Ever since your childhood, you met these people who you thought were talented, and you hooked up with them, and worked with them, and later on they became successful.

JG: Well, some of them did. Richard Branson was successful, but he wasn't an artist. An actress I found in an acting class, called Caroline Cruz Goodall, did well. I put her in a play, and later I ran into her in L.A. and she was playing a part in *Hook*, directed by Steven Spielberg. I was working with Steven at the time. It was like "What a small world!" But artists. Real artists. I've met very few. Tim Burton is one. Malcolm McLaren was another. Sting is another. Annie Lennox. George Harrison. Who else? I met John Waters once. He's a real artist. He originated a new genre in movies. Russ Meyer. I met him once. I'm trying to think... I haven't met many artists. I mean, my mother. She was a real artist. But, you see, they're originals. They do things that haven't been done before. And, what tends to happen to those people, is they usually have a hard time because they're doing something which hasn't been done before.

The people with money don't understand it because it's new. It's misunderstood. But, if they're successful, they get swamped. Everybody wants what they're doing. And they're put under so much pressure, they can't lay their golden eggs anymore. 'Cause you can't do it to order.

MP: Right.

JG: They just have this talent. I mean, when I was a kid I had a talent for drawing. I drew cartoons and I remember that, when I was about eleven, I was drawing something and I thought: "What the hell is this?" I was doing these exaggerated cartoons, and I didn't know where they were coming from. I'd never seen anything like them before. Later, when I was about thirteen or fourteen, I came across drawings by Gillray. James Gillray, and Thomas Rowlandson. They were British cartoonists in the eighteenth century, and my drawings were a bit similar to theirs. But I had no idea where this stuff was coming from. I used to lie on the floor, drawing pictures for hours and hours, and it was like someone else was drawing them.

I remember feeling delighted, like I had a superpower. I was thinking: "Wow! When I grow up I can make money doing this." And then, when I was around fourteen, I saw the drawings of Gerald Scarfe. They were the same as mine! It was uncanny. They were more accomplished, but what he was doing was what I was doing. And I thought: "Shit! I can't do this anymore because Gerald Scarfe is already doing it. If I do it, people will think I'm copying him!" So, I stopped.

MP: But you would have had different stories.

JG: Well, it's the drawings I'm talking about. And there was another guy, called Ralph Steadman, who did the same kind of drawings as well. I often wondered if he was copying Gerald Scarfe or, like me, had come up with it himself.

MP: You should keep all those papers, you know, when you're by the phone, just drawing. You should always keep them. I love those faces that you draw. Keep them on a pile. They're beautiful to see.

JG: They're just doodles.

MP: Yeah, but doodling is still cool.

JG: But, my point about this is: there's something supernatural going on. This style of drawing, which Gerald Scarfe was doing, was very original. Now, why was I doing it? And why was Ralph Steadman doing it?

Did you know six different people invented the aeroplane in the same month? Six different people, in six different parts of the world, all came up with aeroplanes at the same time. But the first ones to get it to fly were the Wright brothers. But, if they'd been a week later, they wouldn't have been the first, and we would never have heard of them.

And this happens with ideas too. I once had a good idea for a play. I was very excited about it, and I sketched it out, wrote it down in one of my notebooks, and I couldn't wait to get started on it. But I was busy with another play, which went into production, and then something else came up, so I didn't get around to it until about a year later.

And just as I started writing it, I went into a bookshop and saw that Fay Weldon had a new book out. It was called *The Life and Loves of a She-Devil*. I like Fay Weldon, so I bought it, and started reading it, and my jaw hit the floor. It was my idea! It was the exact same idea! So, these things happen, and you can't explain it.

MP: Maybe it's people are like, some people are like radios, they can pick up different frequencies…

JG: Well, yeah. There's a theory that the brain is actually a limiter. That it limits, or filters, the information coming in, because there's so much information that, if we absorbed it all, our brains would explode. So, maybe there's all this information swirling around out there and some of us have more holes in our heads than others!

MP: Hahahaha! That's what they mean by 'open-minded.'

JG: Right. But we don't understand anything. It's all such a mystery. You know, the other day, I was watching some interviews with John Lennon on YouTube. And I was listening to his songs and, at the same time, I was reading a wonderful book by Peter Dawkins called *The Shakespeare Enigma*, which lays out all the many, many proofs that the author of the Shakespeare plays was really a group of writers supervised by Sir Francis Bacon. And, at the heart of Bacon's philosophy, which is in all the Shakespeare plays, is the same concept of love as expressed in John Lennon's songs.

So, what I'm saying is, these ideas, which you pick up from the ether, are not only fresh ideas, but can also be ideas from the past that are still of value today. Sometimes an old idea, is a new idea, because we've forgotten it, and we need it, and something is making you pick it up.

MP: Like a new way of doing something old.

JG: Yeah, like that. Malcolm McLaren did that. He'd become fascinated by all kinds of obsolete ideas and, at first, you thought he was joking. These were rotten ideas. But then, it was amazing because he turned them into something new and vital. Have you listened to *Waltz Darling*? His album? You can hear it in that.

When it comes to this question of where do ideas come from, the Ancient Greeks, they really cared about that a lot. The Arts and Sciences. They revered the arts and sciences because they were the sources of civilization. So, they really cared about them, and they had this concept of the Muses. And there's something in that, because the Greeks believed there were ten Muses, and these were goddesses who gave inspiration to chosen mortals. You know, there was one for music, one for painting, one for poetry, there was one for the sciences. And the tenth Muse was Pallas Athena. Well, Athena was born out of the head of Zeus. She wasn't born in the normal way, she came out of his head. So, Athena is thought, do you see? Thought and thinking. And, she was the queen of the Muses, with dominion over the others. And people would be inspired by the Muses. And the Muses come from heaven. And that's how you feel when you're working.

MP: How lovely!

JG: It is, isn't it? Though, often it's drudgery. It's a hard slog, and there's no magic in it at all. You're working, just working, working, working, and then something happens. And you lift off. You're floating. It feels like heaven is flowing through you. And if you do that a lot, too much, that's when you start to go mad. It's like taking drugs for too long. And it makes you sick.

A lot of artists are sickly, or frequently ill – have you noticed that? It takes it out of you. It's not a healthy occupation. It eats you up. It wears you out. You have to make yourself stop or you just get hollowed out.

MP: It can be like that with psychics.

JG: Yes. I've noticed that too. The same thing happens to them. You have to be careful not to do it too much. You have to make yourself go running, or work out at the gym; and take breaks to restore your ch'i. Artists who do it too much crash and burn, like Tennessee Williams, or Philip K. Dick. It wears you out. But real artists do that.

MP: Wow…

JG: But there's not many of them. There are many clever people who are usually more successful than the artists are. They "imitate the best and the rest they memorize." They put 90% of their energy into their careers and only 10% into their work. The Salieris as opposed to the Mozarts. They're not artists, so they have the energy to go out and promote themselves. They're not sucked dry. Not that they don't work hard. They do. They work very hard, but they're not artists. They're imitators.

MP: And Tim is a real artist?

JG: Yeah. Because of his originality. Of course, he's standing on the shoulders of giants. But that's how it works. Mozart took from other composers, and Beethoven took from Mozart. But they bring something original to the table. Like Jimi Hendrix with the guitar. He invented new ways of playing it. And you could see, with Tim, straight out of the gate, with *Pee-wee's Big Adventure*, he was doing something new.

Of course, Paul Reubens, who wrote it and played Pee-wee, was the major creative force, and he's a great talent, and I'm guessing was a fan of the movies of John Waters. But Tim's contribution, as director, was startling. And his artistry just grew from there.

I think it's extraordinary that Tim was – and is – able to work in Hollywood, because, normally they kill artists. But Tim's films are successful. They make money. So, as long as that continues, they will let him do his thing. Did you know all of his movies have made a profit apart from one? No other director has a track record like that.

MP: What was the one that didn't make a profit?

JG: *Ed Wood* – which I think is his best film. But that was manufactured.

MP: What do you mean?

JG: They manufactured the flop. People in Hollywood didn't want it being a hit.

MP: Why not?

JG: Well, I can't prove it, but I think it was for two reasons. The main reason was it was in black and white, and some of the territories the studios sell to, such as Japan and China, won't buy black and white films. So, it was a business reason. If *Ed Wood* had been made in color, or shot in black and white and colorized – which I suggested – there wouldn't have been a problem.

See, the studios didn't want people making black and white films because they'd lose on international sales. But Tim insisted on it being in black and white. So, they had to knock that on the head. And discourage others from making black and white films. A lot of people love black and white. Actors love it, and cinematographers adore it. Can you imagine *Citizen Kane* done in color? It would have been horrible!

MP: Hahaha! Yeah.

JG: And the second reason was… and I've seen this happen to others, like movie stars who ask for too much money… they thought Tim was getting too big for his boots. They wanted to stick a pin in his balloon, and show him who's boss. He'd been too successful. They didn't want to drop him because of what he'd done with his films, and especially *Batman*, was very, very lucrative, and he was a phenomenon – a chicken who laid golden eggs. They just wanted to bring him down a peg, that's all.

MP: Wow. Well, I guess they needed him.

JG: I think so, yes – although they'd never tell *him* that. They prefer the talent to be insecure.

MP: But, I mean, Hollywood wouldn't be able to exist if there weren't at least a few real artists. If you just have these good craftsmen, and imitators, forever and ever, but you never see any geniuses, any true artists, you couldn't sustain it.

JG: Yeah, you need an injection of originality from time to time.

MP: Well, it takes you to another level…

JG: It does. And it gives people stuff to copy. Another real artist was Marlon Brando because he changed the whole way acting was done.

MP: Wow! Yeah, tell us about it.

JG: Well, like I said, it's originality. You get someone doing something nobody's done before and people are fascinated by it, and they copy it. Every actor owes a debt to Marlon Brando. I mean, there were other innovative actors, like Paul

Muni and James Cagney, but he created the way most actors act in movies today.

MP: You told me once he was sitting on a bench, or something, observing people…

JG: Well, yeah. What he did you would think was obvious. And it wasn't a new idea. Stanislavsky had suggested it fifty years before. But he was the first guy to really do it. And when he did it, and people saw it, at first, they said: "What's he doing? He's mumbling. We can't hear what he's saying! And, why is he hiding his face?" But now they say: "Oh, it's obvious."

MP: Like a Zen Master, or a Tibetan Lama. When you have a problem: you're trying and trying to figure out this problem, and you cry and hit your head against the wall about this problem, and then you go to a Lama, tell him your problem. And he's just *Poof!* Something simple that you never thought of, but it's so simple and should be obvious, like: "Well, you could just apologize."

JG: That's it, exactly. Brando was introduced to Stanislavsky by Stella Adler, and he went to the park, sat on a bench, and watched people. This is what Stanislavsky advised actors to do. I mean how obvious is that? But nobody had done it! He studied the people in the park. How they moved. How they spoke to one another. And one of the things he noticed, out of many, was people don't look at each other when they speak. Only occasionally. Unless they're in love, or having a fight.

MP: Yes…

JG: He'd see a loving couple staring into each other's eyes, and when he saw people fighting, they'd be staring into each other's eyes as well. Otherwise, he'd see people talking, talking, talking and only now and again would they make eye contact. So, when he started getting acting work, the director would say: "What are you doing? Look at him. You're speaking to him but you're not looking at him!"

And Marlon Brando said: "But, that's how we are. We only look at people briefly when we talk to them."

So, that's one example. Another thing he noticed was people when they're drunk. What they do is try not to be drunk. So, if you're playing someone who's drunk, you should act like you're trying *not* to be drunk.

MP: Oh wow! They're good psychologists, some of these actors.

JG: Yes, they are. Because they spend a lot of time observing people. It's observation. It's like a painter. A painter spends a lot of time looking at things, and puts a lot of thought into depicting what he sees. So, he shows us things we don't see because we don't spend the time, or the attention, looking. We're busy doing other things. We need artists to show us the world because we're too busy to look at it.

MP: Michelangelo said that when he was doing the David, or any of his sculptures, that the figure was already in the rock. All he had to do was chip away and reveal it.

JG: I think what that is, is letting yourself be guided by your intuition. If you let the quality of the stone guide you, then your figure is not going to be quite what you planned, but it'll be better...

MP: And that leads me to think... Is that what happened with *Mars Attacks!?* Because that seems to me like something like that happened...

JG: Up to a point. I mean, there was a script, and everyone followed the script, but they brought their own skills into interpreting it. So, you've got the qualities and talents of maybe thirty people combining...

MP: And then you have the money-makers who are saying: "Stop! We're gonna cancel!" That also goes into the mix.

JG: Well, yeah. "Executive interference." That's what they call it. Uh, there's an old Hollywood joke. Do you wanna hear it?

MP: Yes.

JG: Okay. It goes: there are three guys and they're lost in a desert. A pilot, a co-pilot and a studio executive. It's very hot and they're lost, and they're walking through the desert, and it's getting hotter and hotter, and they're getting very, very thirsty. They're dehydrating. And then the pilot sees a can of beer in the sand. They can't believe it. They're saved! The pilot picks up the can of beer and pulls off the tab, and says: "This is great! We'll all share it!" And the studio executive says: "Okay, but wait a second. Let me piss in it first."

MP: Hahahaha! They call that executive interference?

JG: Yeah. But it can be good. Not because they're right – though sometimes they are – but because it makes you think again. And, often, you'll come up with something better.

MP: Yeah, you have to be humble to work in that business, don't you? You have to have humility to listen to everyone, and consider everybody's take on things.

JG: Well, it's a balance, isn't it? You need humility for sure. But you don't want to be a wet tissue. You need to defend what you believe is right. The greatest asset you can have, in Hollywood, is the ability to persuade. Writers need that ability to convince producers, executives, and directors to believe in what they've written.

Tim once told me that Warren Skaaren, the writer of *Beetlejuice*, could go into a meeting with a bunch of executives who hated a script, and turn them completely around. Tim's good at persuasion too. And the way he does it is unique, almost invisible. He casts a spell. He, uh, makes you feel like you're detaching from reality. He's like a kid seducing you into playing his game. He reels you into the game and makes you enjoy it so much that you give up control and let yourself be led.

He's not always easy to understand, and that's part of the sorcery. You're trying to understand him, so you open yourself up. Most of us want to understand. And he uses that. See, Tim is so original that you can't second-guess him. You don't know what he's going to say or do next. So, you're kind of destabilized. Your normal defenses don't work. He's like a strange animal you've never met before. So, you become flexible, because you want to understand him. Does that make sense?

MP: Yes, yes.

JG: And then, when you're fully destabilized, he appeals to your inner child. And that's where you connect. That's where you connect with him. Like I said, a lot of people didn't wanna be in *Mars Attacks!* They thought the script was too strange. But when Tim met with them and spoke to them, they became enthused about it. He would get them into that mood of: "Let's be wild and crazy!"

MP: Let's have fun!

JG: Yeah. By appealing to your inner child, he would get you to play. And so, you stop worrying about: "Is this sensible?' Is this good for my career?" You think: well, it's only a movie, who cares? It's a game. And he would create that atmosphere, and that's how he's able to have people − a very disparate group of people − execute his vision. It's a rare skill.

MP: Yeah, it must be great to be around that kind of person. It must feel like you're in and out of a dream.

JG: Yeah. You have to make that jump. You know, like: "Am I gonna join in with the game or not?" But the other thing he has as well, is he's a movie buff. A bit like Steven Spielberg, who's another one like that. Tim has this vast library of movies in his head. And he calls on them a lot. Referencing. Communicating through quoting scenes and characters from movies. It's like a kind of shorthand. Instead of going into a long analysis of the character, he'll say: "He's like a mix between John Wayne and Peter Lorre."

You see, you need that too. It's not enough to be talented; it's not enough to work hard, and it's not enough to be able to beguile the actors and the crew. You also need knowledge. And he has a great knowledge of movies.

After I met him on *Batman,* when he wasn't working, all we did was watch movies.

MP: Really?

JG: Yeah, that's basically all we did. I mean, sometimes we'd go out to eat, but the rest of the time we'd be watching movies.

MP: You were living in a world of movies.

JG: That's all we cared about.

MP: Did you change the script while you were shooting?

JG: Not much. Tim changed a few things. Added a few things. Small changes, that's all. Once you go into production, the director takes over. And, in a sense, the movie is the last draft of the script. And the director guides this draft, which is being written by the cast and crew. Sometimes he'll make a change for budget or schedule reasons, or because an actor wants to do something different, or because, when they put it on the floor, the scene doesn't work too well. And then, later, when you're editing, and putting the film together, you make changes there too. And then it's finished. That's the final draft.

MP: What was cut? Do you remember?

JG: Well, I remember a few things. It's funny, isn't it? I mean, this was over twenty years ago, but I, ha ha… I still remember lines that were cut. Why? I mean, who cares? But they're still in my mind. I guess it was painful to me when they didn't make it into the movie.

One was Scott and Larry's joke about "no kissing on the lips." My own jokes I don't find funny. And it surprises me when people laugh at them. But I enjoy other people's jokes. And the speech by Lukas Haas at the end. That was trimmed. If you want to see the whole speech, it's in the book.

MP: In the *Mars Attacks!* novelization?

JG: Yeah. But Tim may have been right to cut it. I don't know. I liked it at the time. It was a sort of "vision of a new world" speech. Like those speeches that the hero makes at the end of movies like *The Day the Earth Stood Still*, or *War of the Worlds*.

MP: Satire.

JG: Right. The whole thing was a satire.

MP: How would you define satire?

JG: Well, it's making fun of everything. In *Mars Attacks!* we were making fun of American society and old sci-fi movies.

MP: Maybe some people didn't like that.

JG: Maybe. But it was all very harmless.

MP: But you're having a go at the government. And the army, the military. Old hippies and New-Agers. You're having a go at them. And science and scientists, and the media...

JG: Yeah, but...

MP: You know, Sarah Jessica Parker is a TV presenter who has a show about fashion, and...

JG: She's not a proper journalist.

MP: Right. But she gets the story because she's...

JG: Cute. She's cute. Michael J. Fox is the real journalist but he's passed over...

MP: So, you're saying the media is shallow and trivial...

JG: It's just making fun, that's all.

MP: But you're making fun of America, and some Americans probably don't like that.

JG: Okay, but it's also... The movie is also in love with America. It's in love with the common people, with Americans – and with Americana. It's in love with the heartland.

MP: Yes! Like the black kids, like the Jim Brown character, and the Mexican-Americans. And you have Lukas Haas and his granny save the world.

JG: Right. Florence Norris, played by Sylvia Sidney, is a

darling. And he's wonderful, the boy. He's just a lovely young guy.

MP: And a lot of Americans are like this actually.

JG: They are! You've lived in America, so you know. There's a lot of very good people in America. Wonderful people.

MP: Hard-working, generous. Very kind and open-minded and optimistic. You can be what you want to be.

JG: That's right, that's right.

MP: They're really... In America, what I love is the attitude. The 'can do' attitude. You don't have that in Europe where people are more pessimistic. In America, it's like: "Hey, I've got an idea!" And then they say: "Yeah, let's do it!" And they really get on it. They don't think: "Oh, this is gonna go wrong. We don't have the money." They're not thinking of the obstacles. They're thinking about what's gonna go right. Whereas like, here in the UK, most people give up before they start. Maybe it's the weather? Because everything is overcast much of the time here. In San Francisco, and the surrounding mountain area, the weather is great and there's this big open sky. Maybe that's why they have these big open minds. In America, you feel everything is possible.

JG: Yes, and I think that's expressed in the film. The people in the film either think the Martians are gonna be friendly, or they can beat them. Everyone's very positive. And you have a Mexican mariachi band celebrating the victory at the end, which speaks to the diversity of American society, the triumph of the common people, and how everyone's been brought together. This is the American spirit. The positive spirit of America. And, another point, about diversity. That's a key thing in the film too, because it's a key American thing. So, you have the Filipinos who have a farm in the Mid-West and you see the Filipino farmer on a tractor chatting with an old white farmer about the smell of hamburger, and they're buddies.

MP: Barbecue. Someone's having a barbecue.

JG: Right. At the beginning with the burning cows. Well, that speaks to the American dream. He's Filipino, he's got a farm, and he's friendly with his neighbors. And you've got Jim Brown heroically taking on the Martians so the other guys, most of them white, can escape. Everyone's working together. They're not divided. They're Americans! Most of the divisions in society are really a *perception* of division fostered by the media. It's divide and rule.

MP: The plantation system?

JG: Right. Because, if you let people be themselves, they will be friendly with each other. They prefer life that way.

MP: And I can't resist saying this now... American culture, the movies, the music... Rihanna, Kanye West, Tupac, Guns N' Roses, Michael Jackson, The Doors... people love it, and it doesn't only bring people together in America, it does it for the whole world. It's bringing all these different cultures together. Everybody watches American movies, and they love the stars, and they can discuss them and talk about the movies. And lots of people from different parts of the world, they can connect through loving all these different bands and actors and movies, and have a conversation, and be friends, through this American culture coming into the world. That's one great positive thing I see about America. It's actually uniting a lot of the world in a kind of a roundabout way, don't you think?

JG: Yes. I think it's... How it works is you get something which is good, and people like it because it's good, and then what happens is the bad guys hitch a ride on it. They try to co-opt it, control it, and twist it to suit their purposes. So, you have two things, you have the good thing, and then you have the co-option or exploitation of it by the ruling class. So, everything you said is true. Hollywood is a great unifier. But there's also a worm in the apple. The ruling class naturally wants to rule, and they use Hollywood to help them do that.

There are two ways to conquer a country: one is to invade with an army, and the other is to conquer them culturally. So, if you take Japan, for example. First, Japan was conquered militarily. Then, it was conquered culturally with Hollywood movies. And now, today, in Japan, you have a hybrid culture. Half Japanese, half American.

The same thing happened in Britain, although we weren't conquered militarily. In London now everybody says: "Have a nice day!" This is not British, believe me. To British people this statement is ludicrous. And we have proms now. And Halloween. Halloween is an American tradition, not British. Our tradition is Guy Fawkes, November the Fifth – but that's dying out now. People wear baseball caps. Baseball is an American game. The British game is cricket. But that's dying out too. Do you know there are now 300 professional baseball teams in Britain? It's crazy. Do you know Britain's most popular drink?

MP: Tea?

JG: No. Not anymore. Coffee. And the second most popular is Coca-Cola. When I was a kid there was a fish and chip shop on every corner. Now it's McDonalds. See what I mean? It's a cultural takeover. I saw it go into high gear during the 70's, when Hollywood got control of all the British cinemas, and forced the collapse of the British film industry. It's a cultural take over. And once you've taken over the culture of a country, you've conquered it permanently.

MP: That's why I'm wondering about Hollywood. It's like, it's everywhere in the world.

JG: Yeah, they've got over 80% of the world's film market.

MP: How did they do that? How did they get that, do you know? They had to be very rich. Were they always so rich, Hollywood?

JG: They were fantastically rich.

MP: From the beginning?

JG: Well no, not from the beginning. If you go back before World War One, it was the British film industry that was the biggest in the world. Because Britain had the Empire "upon which the sun never set."

MP: Hahaha!

JG: We had an empire that controlled a third of the world.

And, we developed films and cinemas before anyone else. It was the British who made the first narrative film – a film with a story. And the first to develop ways to process film footage, on nitrate and celluloid film stock. And, like Hollywood today, we sent out our films to the colonies, and people watched them and liked them. And there was no language barrier because the films were silent.

So, we were the number one film industry up until 1914. Then the Great War happened and wiped us out. And that's when the Americans picked up the ball and ran with it. They had people like D.W. Griffiths, Cecil B. Demille, and Alan Dwan and, later, British immigrants like Charlie Chaplin who made innovations and developed the film industry.

The Americans first started making feature films in New York and Chicago. Then, to avoid license fees, and to benefit from the sunshine, they moved out to California and founded a filmmaking colony in Hollywood. And they were very successful. They made a lot of money. And it was primarily a Jewish enterprise. See, it was hard for Jews, at that time, to get into other industries because of anti-Semitism, which was very common back then. All the established industries were owned and controlled by anti-Semites. And Jews were banned from the golf clubs where a lot of these captains of industry did their business deals. But there was nothing to stop them making movies. In fact, the establishment thought 'the flickers' were a passing fad. But, of course, these clever Jewish guys, like Louis B. Meyer, Jesse Lasky, Sam Goldwyn, Adolph Zukor, Carl Laemmle, William Fox, and Harry Cohn proved them wrong.

And then, sometime in the 20's... I think it was to do with a movie called *Greed* by Erich von Stroheim, which went way over budget and made a big loss. And after that, the investors decided movies were too important to be made by directors, and they started setting up the studio system.

MP: Can you explain the studio system?

JG: Sure. Up until about 1926, movies were made by directors, okay? The director would write the scenario, get the actors and crew together, operate the camera, cut the film – he'd do everything. Charlie Chaplin did all that, plus he starred in his films *and* wrote the music. But some of these directors wasted a lot of the investors' money, so they organized a control system, along the lines of a garment factory, with departments.

They set up a story department for scripts, a camera department, an art department to take care of the sets and costumes, a casting department to choose the actors, an editing department, and a marketing and distribution department. So, they didn't really need directors after that because films were made by these departments. But they kept the position of director because people were used to it, and you still needed someone to call action and cut, and to watch what the actors were doing. To stand in for the audience. But that was the end of film directors, in the sense of the film director making the film.

MP: Wow. But most people think directors *do* make the film.

JG: Well, yeah. And directors did start to make a comeback in the 50's after the *U.S. v. Paramount* decision, which partly broke up the studio system. And there was the French New Wave in the 60's, when guys like Truffault, Eric Rohmer, and Jean-Luc Godard wrote and directed movies they produced themselves. And this inspired guys like Woody Allen and

John Cassavetes in the States, to write and direct. And they called these guys 'auteurs,' which means authors, which is fair enough. But they weren't authors like the silent movie directors were. Other people did the filming, editing, and production design.

I mean, Tim Burton contributes a lot more to his movies than most directors do, but he doesn't call himself an 'auteur.' The only director of recent times who could call himself that was Russ Meyer, because he did everything. But the main reason people think directors make films is, I think, because of marketing. Because, when a movie is released, the studio sends the director out to represent it to the press. And naturally, when he's interviewed, he calls it 'my film.' So, people think he made it.

MP: I see. Okay, so here's another question. Something I've always wondered about. Can you explain how the stars manage to make such good money deals?

JG: Yes, well that's because... Well, let's go back to the origins of that. It started back in the Silent Era. *The Biograph Girl.* Did you ever hear of the Biograph girl?

MP: No.

JG: Well, in the early days, the film companies advertised their films by publicizing the name of the company. "Next week, we've got the new Goldwyn picture. Or the new Biograph picture." And people would go and see it, and they'd say: "Oh, I love that girl in the Biograph picture. The Biograph girl." And they'd say: "Oh, have you seen the new Biograph girl movie?" They went because the Biograph girl was in it.

Not because it was a Biograph film. They loved Mary Pickford. They didn't know her name, but they knew her face. And they'd go see her films. They didn't care about the name of the movie company.

MP: Yeah!

JG: And the boss of the company, William Dickson, got fed up with it. He wanted his company brand to be famous, not the actors. And when Mary Pickford asked him for billing and more money, he said no. So, Mary Pickford, who was a great innovator, refused to go to work.

And the theater owners started hitting up the company saying "Where's the new *Biograph Girl* film? Where is it? Everybody wants to see it." There was a demand for it. So, William Dickson went back to her and agreed to reveal her name, and pay her more. And she doubled down. She demanded that his other lead actress got billing too. So, the Biograph girl was revealed as Mary Pickford, and their other nameless star was revealed as Florence Lawrence. This started an avalanche. All the other film companies followed suit, and that's how the star system started.

And, following Mary Pickford's example, the stars fought for more money. And because movies became more popular, as they got better and better – there was no TV then – money poured into the film companies, and the stars had the leverage to get some of that money for themselves.

And, even though they were paying a lot to the stars, the companies got so rich they built huge complexes of soundstages, and set up their own acting schools, and signed actors to seven-year contracts, and trained them to be stars. They opened a publicity department to get their pictures in the papers and magazines. They did this with countless actors during the 30's and 40's and 50's. And they got writers to craft vehicles for them.

If the audience liked an actor in a certain role, the studio would make him play the same character in different movies. Like Cary Grant, for example. In an interview, Cary Grant said to the interviewer: "I wish I was Cary Grant. I would love to be like him." Because he wasn't like that at all. He was playing a character. His real name was Archibald Leach and he was an entirely different person.

John Wayne became famous as a cowboy in *Stagecoach*, directed by John Ford. So, after that, he played cowboys. And not different cowboys, the same cowboy. And, later on, he played the same character in a different costume, in war movies. They were typecast. The actors were typecast.

MP: Aha.

JG: They did the same with some of the directors. 'The Lubitsch Touch.' That was a publicity campaign creating a brand that equated Ernst Lubitsch with light comedies. The publicity department did the same with Alfred Hitchcock. They invented the term 'thriller' and Hitchcock was assigned to oversee these creepy, suspense films. He complained because he preferred romantic comedies and musicals but, like the actors, he was typecast. He had to do 'thrillers.' That was the Hitchcock brand that the studio had created to push sales.

So, that's how it worked. Stars attracted people to the movie theaters, so the studio bosses put a lot of effort into creating stars. And they didn't all have to be actors. They could be directors, even animals, like Rin-Tin-Tin, who was a dog. Paramount Pictures made Edith Head into a star. She was a costume designer. This happened because women would watch a film and say: "Oh, I like that dress. I wish I had one like that."

And this developed into a lucrative sideline – pattern selling. In the thirties and forties, many people made their own clothes by buying patterns from the shop and cutting and sewing the fabric themselves. So, the studios promoted Edith Head, had their female stars model her dresses in the movies, and made money selling the patterns. Glamour. They were selling glamour.

MP: I think you told me once the meaning of the word *glamour*?

JG: It was a magic spell that made you beautiful. The glamour spell.

MP: Ah, illusion. Now, I'd like to ask you about the book. The *Mars Attacks!* book.

JG: The novelization?

MP: Yes.

JG: Okay, let's see. We were near the end of post-production – or maybe we'd finished post-production – and I got a call from somebody at Warner Bros, saying that they were going to do the novelization of *Mars Attacks!* And, they were gonna send me a contract to sign, and some money. I think, it was about $1,500. And I said: "What do you mean the novelization?" And they said: "Well, we always do novelizations of our movies."

So, I thought: Wait a minute, why can't I do it?

And they said: "No, no, you don't wanna do it. It's just a little silly thing. We sell a few of them, but it's not serious. It's just a spin off. Some people like to buy the novelization." So, I said: "I'd like to do it." And they said: "Well, that's not normal, we don't do that. We have novelizers to do the novelizations." I said: "Well, is there anything against me writing it?" And they said: "You can't do it. You've never done it before, and we have to have it in a month. Because it has to come out at the same time as the film."

And I said: "No problem. I can do it in a month." I mean, I had no idea if I could do it. I'd never done it before. But I didn't like the idea of somebody else writing it. But they didn't want this, and they said they'd get back to me.

So, I called Jeff Field, my agent, and found out that I had first refusal. It was in my contract. They couldn't give the novelization to someone else without my permission.

And while that was going on, I ran into Larry Karazewski, who had done a bit of work on *Mars Attacks!* He was in a café on Melrose, having coffee with his partner, Scott. I was just walking by and saw them. So, I went in to say "Hi." And Larry said: "I heard you wanna do the novelization." I mean, the gossip in Hollywood is amazing! Everything gets around. If you say anything, everybody's heard it by the next day.

MP: Hahahaha!

JG: And I said: "Yeah, I want to do the novelization." And he said: "No, you don't want to do it. It's a waste of time. You should let them do it. Nobody reads it. Nobody cares about the novelization."

MP: Because they wanted to do it?

JG: No, no. They just said: "It's a lot of work. Why do it? You're not getting anything out of it."

MP: But it's a great book. I love that book.

JG: Well, thank you. But they were right really. Nobody cares about the novelization. No one takes it seriously. I just felt I should do it. So, I asked my agent to tell them I was exercising my right to do it, and they had to let me do it.

MG: Yes!

JG: Now, I'd never written a novel before, and I only had a month. So, it was a bit hair-raising. But I knew the whole movie. I had it all in my head, right? So, I thought: "I'll get a secretary, a typist, and I'll just dictate." Now, at the time, I was attracted to an actress named Amber, and we went out to dinner. But she wasn't much interested in me. However, she had this nice friend called Apryl Runnells who needed a job. So, I said: "Can you type?"

And she said: "Yeah. I can type really fast."

So, for three weeks, Apryl came over to my flat every day, and we wrote the book.

MP: How many hours a day?

JG: All day. She would arrive at 10 a.m. and leave at six or seven. And, after she left, I'd grab a bite to eat, and then prepare everything for the next day.

MP: She must have loved it.

JG: She did enjoy it, yeah. She was great. I remember she made me a custom tape of songs she liked. She was really sweet. So, we finished it, and I sent it in, and I got a call saying: "It's too long. We told you 200 pages."

And I said: "But it *is* 200 pages."

And she said: "No, no! You've delivered 200 manuscript pages, and it's all single-spaced. This works out, in book form, as 300 pages!"

So, I said: "Is that a problem?"

She said: "Well, no, but we don't like it. It's not what we asked for, and it's not what we're used to."

So, they weren't happy with it, but there was no time, so they sent it to the book company, which was called Sphere, and they designed a cover and printed it.

And I asked them why didn't they use Warner Books? Why use Sphere? And they said because Warner Books was too expensive. They got a better deal at Sphere. This was one of those head-scratchers. You know, Time Warner was this big conglomerate, always talking about the advantages of 'vertical integration' and 'synergy.' But they were always going to outside companies because they were cheaper and better!

MP: So, the book includes things that aren't in the movie?

JG: Yeah, it gives you more information, more details, about the characters, and scenes that didn't make into the film. If you have any questions about the movie, you can find the answers in the book.

MP: On the internet, it's being sold for £24.

JG: Is it?

MP: The used version. New it is £63.

JG: No!

MP: Yeah!

JG: Wow. That's a lot to pay for that!

MP: Yeah, and the *Mars Attacks!* dolls are going for about £400.

JG: Oh God! I should have kept mine.

MP: So, I was wondering... I've seen on YouTube, a lot of people making comments under these *Mars Attacks!* clips. A lot of them watched the film when they were kids. And they were terrified. It gave them nightmares. There was one girl who said: "I'm twenty-three and I was so terrified when I was a little kid. But every day I watch a little bit and I'm so happy I can do it now." What's that all about, do you think?

JG: Hah! Yeah, I think that was a common experience. I knew a lovely young woman named Jacqui de la Fontaine, who lived near me in Whitley Heights. And she had a daughter called Gia. Gia's father was Gio Coppola, the son of Francis Ford Coppola. It's a tragic story. Gio died in a boating accident before Gia was born, so she never got to know her father. Very sad. Anyway, in 1996, Gia was about eight, and she wanted to go see *Mars Attacks!* Now, she was a delightful kid. Very lively. Full of energy. Absolutely adorable. So, I said I'd take her and Jacqui to see it. It was playing at a movie theater on Hollywood Boulevard.

So, we went. And we watched it. And when it was over, we came out, and Gia was very quiet. This wasn't like her. She was normally very lively and chatty. And her mom asked her if she was all right. But she shook her head and wouldn't speak.

Anyhow, the next day, I got a call from Jacqui, and she was upset. She said Gia had been having nightmares all night, and it was all my fault! I should have warned her that the movie was violent and scary. I should have told her that it wasn't suitable for children.

Well, that took me aback because the truth was, I'd never thought about whether it was suitable for children. I'd never thought about that at all. But now I could see her point. I remembered when I was eight years old and saw *The Lost World*, which scared me to death. And that was only a few dinosaurs. So, I felt bad. The last thing I wanted to do was upset little Gia. I felt terrible. So, I... I apologized as best I could. But Jacqui wasn't having it. She was really angry with me. She really made me feel like a jerk.

But a couple of days later, Jacqui called and she said: "Gia wants to speak to you."

MP: Oh really?

JG: Yeah. And I was a bit nervous. I didn't know what she was going to say. I said: "Hello Gia, how are you?" And she said: "Please can we go see the film again?"

MP: Hahahaha! And what did her mother say?

JG: Well, her mother was just as bewildered as I was.

MP: Did you take her to see it?

JG: No, I was too busy at that time. That's when I was making *The Treat*. But she got some of her relatives to take her.

MP: Yeah, I suppose, for children of that age, it can seem scary. I watched it when I was nineteen, and for me it was just, like, so funny. Hahaha! But many comments go something like this: "This terrified me as a kid but now I just find it hilarious! It's my favorite movie!"

JG: Yeah, it seems to traumatize them when they're eight or nine, and yet it gives them something they want. So, they go back to get more of it. I don't know what it is. But, it may be something to do with the development of the psyche. We need to be introduced to horrific things, and it's disturbing the first time it happens because we're not prepared for it. But, deep down, you need to prepare your emotional equipment for this, so you want to see it again and again and again.

MP: Yeah…

JG: Because you're building emotional muscles to deal with fear and adversity.

MP: Yeah, because I mean, these things could happen in real life.

JG: I hope not!

MP: But there are wars. Shocking things happen. And we need to be able to face them. Not Martians necessarily, hahaha! But you know what I mean…

JG: Yeah. It's the same reason people like horror films. On the face of it, it's strange that people pay money to go and watch horror movies where all kinds of horrible and frightening things happen. But it's actually nourishing.

MP: Yeah. They should show *Mars Attacks!* in schools.

JG: They'll never do that.

MP: Why not? It's educational!

JG: Hahaha!

MP: What about the editing of *Mars Attacks!*?

JG: Well, I remember the editing. Chris Lebenzon. He was the editor. A very nice guy. Very collaborative. He'd done the cutting on *Batman Returns* and *Ed Wood*. He's a fine editor, and a pleasure to work with. A very genial guy.

On *Mars Attacks!* it was being done on Avid, which was a new invention at that time. It's all digital. All the takes are digitized, so then you can select them and move them around, place them where you want, trim them, whatever, and play back what you've just cut. It was a great technology. But it was all new, and Chris was learning how to use it, which added to the stress.

But it was better and quicker than cutting a work print, a celluloid work print, and working on a Steenbeck. A big step forward. But I remember Chris Lebenzon really sweating bullets, learning how to use it.

MP: Gosh, on the job!

JG: Yeah, but he mastered it.

MP: What was it like when the movie was finished? Did you go to the wrap party?

JG: No, I was too busy on *The Treat*. But I talked to Tim, to say I wasn't going, and he said he didn't want to go either. He was exhausted. He was sick of the movie business. He told me: "I don't wanna do this anymore." He was really depressed. So, Lisa-Marie persuaded him to go to India for a holiday.

So, they went, and Warner Bros were panicking because they couldn't get a hold of him. They were doing the marketing; they were preparing for the release, and I was getting phone calls from journalists, talking to me about the movie because they couldn't get Tim.

And when he got back from India, he was still pretty depressed, and, I don't know, but, at that time, I don't think he was on good terms with the studio. Maybe that's another reason why the campaign was so poor.

MP: That's such a shame, because the movie was so good!

JG: Karmic winds.

MP: What do you mean?

JG: The karmic winds were blowing against us.

MP: Why do you think that was?

JG: At the time, I didn't know. But now I think, for whatever reason, the powers-that-be didn't like *Mars Attacks!*

And I think they wanted to punish Tim Burton for making it. Which they did later on, by canceling *Superman Lives,* which was his next project, and would have been something very special.

MP: Well, you were punished too, weren't you?

JG: I was punished more than he was. After *Mars Attacks!* came out, it was all over for me. That was the end of my career as a screenwriter. The phone stopped ringing. I was never offered another gig. Everything went downhill after that.

It's like Snakes and Ladders. I'd climbed to the top of the ladder – or near the top – in Hollywood, and then I slipped down a snake. Right down to the bottom again. And, to make matters worse, I got Hepatitis C. I was really sick. And the doctors gave me three to five years to live.

MP: Wow. When was that?

JG: 1998.

MP: Well, you're still alive!

JG: I guess they were wrong.

MP: Tim was the only one who visited you after you got sick, wasn't he?

JG: Yeah. After I got sick with Hep C, my Hollywood friends vanished in the haze. Mind you, I went back to England, and I wasn't very communicative, so my friends probably thought

I had vanished in the haze! Tim kept in touch, though, and later on I did a little work for him on *Corpse Bride*.

MP: When did you get better?

JG: 2018.

MP: 2018? So, you were sick for twenty years?

JG: Yeah. It wasn't fun. And, during that time, both my parents died.

MP: Oh.

JG: But suffering is good for the artist. Haha. It splits you off from the herd. It makes you an outsider. And it makes you think. You do a lot of thinking. Percy Bysshe Shelley said: "You learn in suffering what you teach in song." And I think that's true. It's the same principle as the 'wounded healer.'

And, although, during those twenty years, I was too ill, and too brain-fogged, to work, I could read. And reading is thinking with other people's thoughts. So, I did that. I read all the time. I read hundreds of books.

That's what got me through the illness. And I was fighting the virus every day. I refused to succumb to it – and that gave me a sense of purpose. And, when I got better, I found it much easier not to be seduced by group-think.

MP: Yeah, that makes me ask you a question. This goes through all your work – thinking for yourself. It's like a theme in all your work.

JG: Is it?

MP: I think so, yes. It's like you're urging people to be free-thinkers. It seems to me, you believe that these are the people who make a difference in the world.

JG: Well, they're the *only* people who make a difference in the world. They are the ones who give us progress. I mean, if you look at all the inventors, the people who invented wonderful things like bicycles and electricity, they're all people who thought for themselves. You might think inventing the bicycle is science, by the way, but it's not, it's art. It's creative. What we call scientific research is actually an art. Medicine is an art.

Art, in the wide sense of the word, is having ideas. It's thinking. It's Minerva, the chief of all the Muses. Science is knowledge, the body of work accumulated by artists. And artists need science. They need knowledge. And they need technology too. You need all three. Art, Science and Craft.

If you go back to Renaissance times, they never made a difference between the arts, crafts, and sciences because they're inseparable.

MP: Right.

JG: The ruling class divided them. It used the schools to put them in different compartments. They saw people in terms of their use value. It's the same today. "Human resources." What a chilling term that is! They wanted everyone to specialize so they only learn one thing. Only do one thing, so they never get to see the big picture. That way, they can be manipulated.

MP: It's like in the medical industry, they divide this organ from that organ. You have the heart or cardiology specialist divided from the liver or hepatology specialist. Everybody's divided into different departments, which is the opposite of how Eastern medicine works... Like Tibetan, or Chinese medicine, Japanese medicine, or Ayurveda.

JG: Yeah, they're holistic, which is better. Less harmful, and more effective. But allopathic medicine – western medicine – which, apart from surgery, is based on poisons, is a massive industry. Bigger than the oil industry. It's very powerful. And they won't give up their power easily.

You see, they want us to believe in experts. The experts are the best people to make the decisions. And we have to obey them because they have more qualifications. Actually, they are *less* qualified because they're blinkered. They only know about their own little compartment. And, because of this, they're actually dangerous. Especially in medicine. Did you know there were two doctors' strikes in Israel? And, both times, the death rate went down!

MP: Yes, it's like: "Don't trust yourself but go and consult an expert." Something like that...

JG: Yes. That's the basic message of *Mars Attacks!* Don't trust the experts. But this probably isn't what they want coming out of Hollywood. They want people to believe in the experts.

MP: Can I just make one comment?

JG: Uhuh?

MP: What you are saying the message of *Mars Attacks!* is is what the great Zen Master Shunryu Suzuki Roshi said in his book *Zen Mind, Beginner's Mind*. He said, at the beginning of the book: "In the beginner's mind there are many possibilities, but in the expert's mind there are few."

JG: Ah!

MP: And it's almost like you and Tim Burton are like these guys with a beginner's mind, you know? That is open. And you can go anywhere, and it's like that's where all the possibilities lie. And in the expert's mind, he's so indoctrinated by his being an expert, it's very limited.

JG: Yeah. One of the things I've always noticed about experts, whether academics, or dentists, or lawyers, is their imagination has been suppressed. They don't even *want* to think outside the box. And I think that's what schools and colleges do to people. They suppress their imagination, which is bad because we need our imagination. It's a vital part of our cognitive equipment. It's an important part of how we think.

MP: You also reminded me of another quote by Akong Tulku Rinpoche: "Only the impossible is worth doing."

JG: Oh, that's inspiring, isn't it? Akong Rinpoche, the great Tibetan Lama. And, coming from him... I mean, Akong Rinpoche *did* do the impossible, didn't he? He's talking from personal experience. He's a person who did extraordinary things. And we can *all* do extraordinary things if we can just set ourselves free. Do you know something interesting?

MP: What?

JG: A lot of people who've done extraordinary things were dyslexic.

MP: Really?

JG: Yes. Richard Branson, for example. Marlon Brando was dyslexic. Actually, I think Tim Burton's a bit dyslexic.

I read a magazine article about a study that was done. These researchers interviewed fifty billionaires. They gave them a questionnaire to fill out. The idea was to see if they shared any common characteristics. And the result was surprising. Twenty-eight percent were dyslexic, and had left school early.

The conclusion the magazine writer made was that the success of these billionaires was because they were compensating for their handicap. They were motivated to work harder and be more pushy than other people. But I'm not sure about that. I think it's more likely that, having dyslexia, they were hopeless at schoolwork and were rejected by their teachers, so they had to start thinking for themselves. And, naturally, they hated school, so they left as soon as they could. Most of these dyslexic billionaires left school at fifteen or sixteen. So, they weren't indoctrinated, you see?

MP: Right.

JG: Much of our school teaching is based on the Prussian education system, which was introduced under Frederick the Great. And his purpose was to turn kids into soldiers. He wanted to have the best army in Europe. So, the system was designed to train people to follow orders.

It's really training, not education. Because you're not encouraged to think. They don't teach the Socratic method. Everybody's trained like dogs, to follow orders and do tricks. Thinking for yourself is discouraged, even punished.

MP: You know, I was looking on YouTube and on Facebook at the comments about the film. And people love it! They have all these conversations about it, and get excited about it. "It's my favorite movie ever!" You see that a lot. I hardly saw any comments that were critical. Some guys even have tattoos, tattoos of the Martians...

JG: Really?

MP: Yeah!

JG: They must be nuts!

MP: No, they love it.

JG: Well, Hollywood is not a democracy. It's not even a meritocracy. It's an oligarchic dictatorship. You can make a movie that's popular and makes a profit, but if the powers-that-be don't like it, you're outta here! Sayonara!

MP: My God... Maybe, I mean, when you were doing *Mars Attacks!* you weren't thinking about challenging the powers-that-be, were you?

JG: No. Not at all.

MP: You were just making a fun movie, which happened to turn out to be a kind of anti-propaganda.

JG: Hm.

MP: I mean, in a Sylvester Stallone movie, he might kill, like, forty people, right? He's going behind enemy lines and killing Russians or whatever, and it gets the boys excited. They'll watch it and say: "Oh yeah, I wanna join the marines!" But in *Mars Attacks!* the army is useless. The air force is useless. And the soldier played by Jack Black gets disintegrated. No recruitment there! Hahaha!

JG: Yeah, yeah, yeah. That was supposed to be funny but…

MP: They don't see it that way. To them it's *not* a joke.

JG: Yeah. Maybe so. But, whatever the reason, somebody high up didn't like it. Tim got punished. I was frozen out. Even though the movie was a hit. I mean, people think the studios only care about money. But it's not true. They're also political, and have been for some time.

Franklin D. Roosevelt, for example, gave tax advantages to Warner Bros, and later other studios, for making anti-German movies to encourage Americans to join in the Second World War, which the American people didn't want to do. And the studios still make blatant propaganda films like *Charlie Wilson's War* or *Zero Dark Thirty*. Hollywood is a powerful public relations tool. The biggest in the world.

And, ultimately, Hollywood is controlled by Wall Street and the New York Fed. It's controlled by the guys in our current banking system who create the currency. These are the people the studio presidents report to. The same guys Franklin D. Roosevelt reported to.

And one of the things that happened in the last ten years is Chinese money going into Hollywood. China is a communist dictatorship. It has a slave labor system. It kills people for their organs. You have the Falong Gong where they tell us one and a half million people were killed for organ harvesting. They've put over a million Muslims in re-education camps.

MP: Well, they massacred the Tibetans, including Lamas and monastics. They destroyed ancient Buddhist monasteries...

JG: Yes, they hate religion. Under communism they want you to worship the state. The Romans tried to do this. They built temples to the Emperor Augustus and tried to get the Jews to worship the Roman emperor as a god. But it didn't work. And the Chinese Communist Party won't work either. It's doomed to failure, like the Soviet Union.

I've heard the Chinese Communist Party is ruled by an oligarchy of a hundred wealthy families. And these guys are rich, rich, rich, rich. And they're brutal. Just as brutal as the Romans were, who also had a slave system with patricians at the top. Your iPhone can be made very cheaply, because the people who make them get thirty cents an hour. And some of the assembly work requires tiny fingers, so they use children.

You have eight-year old children working in the factories. And the conditions are harsh. The men and women are separated. The men in one block, and the women in another. They're not allowed to meet. And they work all the time. And sometimes it gets so bad, they want to kill themselves. So, there are guards to watch them, and they have suicide nets to catch people if they jump off the high places.

So, you have this massive nation of almost one and a half billion people – which is more than all the people in the whole of Africa – and it's almost as bad as *1984*: George Orwell's vision of a future ruled by communists. But the bankers are happy because their trans-national corporations are getting cheap labor, and making money, and money is power. They're in control.

When you think about it, things haven't changed that much since Roman times.

MP: Oh, my God...

JG: The banks and the multinationals love socialism. It was the bankers who started socialism in the first place. They funded Karl Marx to write *Das Kapital* and *The Communist Manifesto*. They funded and trained Lenin and Trotsky. The Russian Revolution wasn't a revolution, it was a takeover of Russia by the banks. Lenin's first act, when he gained power, was to set up a central bank. That was his first decree.

At school, we were told, as kids at school, that socialism was "fair shares for all." And we believed it. Why wouldn't we? It sounded good. It sounded like a great system that everyone should follow. It sounded fair. Most young people believe in socialism because that's what they're told. When I was eighteen, I joined the Labour Party – which was a socialist party – because I thought things should be fair.

We were taught, as children, to love Robin Hood, who took from the rich and gave to the poor. We used to watch a TV series called *Robin Hood*, starring Richard Greene. The sexy actress playing Maid Marion was the first woman I fell in love with.

"Feared by the bad, loved by the good! Robin Hood, Robin Hood, Robin Hood!"

That was the chorus of the theme song. And it went in deep. And it's still going on now, this indoctrination. But it's a deception. A grand deception. Because socialism is, in reality, a way for the rich to rob the poor. It's the opposite of what they say it is.

Socialism is the government controlling the people. Libertarianism is the people controlling the government. And it's an age-old war. It's been going on for two thousand years. One of the first people to speak about it was the Chinese sage, Confucius – back in 400 BC. He called the two systems: *Legalistic Government* and *Libertarian Government.*

Under a Libertarian Government, you have very few rules. People are free to do what they want. The only rules are: don't kill, don't steal, don't hurt other people, and honor your agreements.

MP: Don't have sexual misconduct?

JG: Sure. Don't have sexual misconduct because it hurts people. So, don't do it. But, as long as you don't hurt people, you can do what you want. That's Libertarianism.

Socialism, well that's different. Socialism is very complicated. Because it's a deception. When you want to deceive people, you bamboozle them. You confuse them with language – like the legal and the medical professions, who have devised their own languages to confuse their customers.

Language should be for the communication of meaning. But scam-artists use it to obscure meaning – to mislead and manipulate. So, as you would expect in a scam operation, socialism has many different names, such as: communism, fascism, authoritarianism, Marxism, corporatism, autocracy, oligarchy, plutocracy, bolshevism, monarchism, feudalism, dictatorship, technocracy... all these different names.

But they're all the same thing. Confucius called it *Legalism*. Legalistic government. He called it that because its key characteristic is legislation, in other words: rules. Rules, rules, rules, rules, rules. Thousands of rules. Tens of thousands of rules. You tie everyone up with rules.

And now the government, which works for the ruling class, has this immense apparatus for spying on people. It's getting more and more like George Orwell's Big Brother. "Big Brother is Watching You."

The more rules, the more legalistic, a government is, the more socialist it is.

MP: Wow. Obviously, there is a rich ruling class still around. And if we had socialism, as they describe it to us, everybody would have a fair share, but in reality, you have slaves killing themselves, and the super-rich ruling class controlling the whole process. So, nothing changes. It becomes even worse. People are allowing the ruling class to still lead them by not looking at what is actually happening. Instead, they believe what they read in the newspapers... and what's on television.

JG: Right.

MP: Yes. So, basically, everything we hear in the media is propaganda.

JG: That's it.

MP: And they want to impose socialism on people because it creates more wealth for them, and the power is centralized in their hands.

JG: Exactly. It's easy for the banks to do this because they create the currency. And they use it to buy everything. They buy control of the education system, the medical industry, the politicians, the media – everything of importance.

I'm old enough to remember the *Village Voice* and *Rolling Stone* magazine when they were libertarian. When I was about ten, we went with my father to America. We went to New York, San Francisco, all over the place. And the *Village Voice* was this underground newspaper, and it was exposing government scandals, and campaigning against the Vietnam War, and urging people to think for themselves. *Rolling Stone* was the same.

But what happened was, the big money came in and put an end to it. And they both started producing the same socialist twaddle as everyone else. As a result, the *Village Voice* gradually lost more and more readers until it went bust.

Socialism has always been imposed using deception. Deception is a weapon. Sun Tsu, in the *Art of War*, says all wars are won by deception. And socialism is a war against the people by the ruling class.

So, now, today, *Rolling Stone* promotes political correctness and so-called liberal values. But this is a deception. It's anti-liberal. The liberals of the nineteenth century were libertarians. They fought, and died for, freedom of speech. But the liberals of today are trying to restrict and censor speech. They're not liberals, they're socialists. But they call themselves liberals to fool the public. Corrupting the meanings of words is what they do.

George Orwell anticipated this in *1984*. You have The Ministry of Truth – which Orwell based on the BBC – which is really the Ministry of Propaganda. And the hero of *1984*, Winston Smith, works there, and one of his jobs is to erase words from the dictionary.

MP: It's been proven already. Propaganda was used in the Second World War. You know, a lot of it. If you look at historical documentaries…

JG: Sure. I remember seeing a video showing newspapers from 1914. In one of the newspapers… on the cover of the *Daily Mail*, I think it was, there was a cartoon of Kaiser Wilhelm, the king of Germany, spearing babies with a bayonet. The story was that the Germans were in Belgium killing babies with bayonets. It was completely untrue. Completely made up. But people believed it! The ruling class was trying to get people to hate the Germans and volunteer to join up and fight the First World War.

And, later, the owner of the *Daily Mail*, was 'ennobled.' He was made a lord – Lord Northcliffe. So that's what they do.

MP: Yes, so, so, so, in effect, when they see the opportunity, when there's something popular, influential, like this *Village Voice* was among the people, and when it's owned maybe by a group of free, independent-thinking people, independent journalists, trying to do something good, then these ruling class people buy it to use it for their propaganda.

JG: That's it.

MP: I wonder why these people sell it though? It's a powerful tool that can be misused…

JG: They're forced into selling it.

MP: Because they don't have enough money? What's the reason?

JG: There are all kinds of ways you can force a publication, or any business, to sell. And, if you can't, you can pass legislation to order a business to sell. This happened with the BBC. Back in, I think, 1937, the BBC was an independent company. But then the government wanted to buy it for their own purposes. The BBC refused to sell, so the government passed a law that ordered them to sell it.

In Hollywood, in the 90's, there was an independent film company called Samuel Goldwyn Films. A small independent company, founded by Sam Goldwyn Jr., making intelligent, interesting films. They did a lot of the Merchant Ivory Films, based on books by authors like E.M. Forster, which were quite high-brow but popular.

But Sam Goldwyn Jr. lost money on a few films and was strapped for cash and one of the studios made him an offer. They said he could continue running the company, and make the movies he wanted, if he sold the company to them. So, he did it. He sold his company to them, and they fired him.

MP: Jesus! That's terrible.

JG: There's a Japanese saying: "Business is war." And wars are won by deception. The same thing happened to PolyGram in the UK. Well, not quite the same thing.

PolyGram was a good Anglo/Dutch movie studio, owned by Phillips. It was run by a brilliant producer named Michael Kuhn. He was doing co-productions with American film companies, and also funding and releasing some good British films. Hollywood didn't like this. So, Universal Studios made Phillips an offer they couldn't refuse. They offered the board of Phillips $5 billion – ten times more than PolyGram was worth. It was so much money, they couldn't resist it. So, they sold PolyGram to Universal, who promptly shut it down.

MP: So, they have unlimited amounts of money?

JG: Sure. They *print* the money!

MP: Okay, so let's move on. Uh, what are your thoughts about Danny Elfman, who composed the music?

JG: Oh, he's great. A great film composer. Very talented and very hard-working. And he must have done something good in a previous life because he got Bridget Fonda. He married Bridget Fonda! How lucky can you get? But he's a great guy. He's been through the mill. He's smart and battle-scarred. I don't know if he's got Irish blood in him – maybe Scottish – but he's like one of those warriors in *Braveheart*. He gave me some good advice once.

MP: What was it?

JG: I can't say. It's confidential.

MP: I love his music in *Mars Attacks!*

JG: His music is brilliant. And, *Oingo Boingo*, his band, was something different. It was original. He's a real artist. Tim was clever to ask him to write the score for *Pee-wee's Big Adventure*.

MP: It's the one I never saw. Is it good?

JG: It's great! Warner's liked Paul Reubens' script and signed to make the movie, but I don't think they cared about it much. It was low budget. About $6m. They had trouble finding a director for it until Shelley Duvall, who'd worked on Tim's short film *Frankenweenie*, told Paul Reubens that Tim would be great for it. And they couldn't find anyone to direct it. I think probably because it was a low-budget kids' film and it was weird.

MP: Is Shelley Duvall the one who played Jack Nicholson's wife in *The Shining*?

JG: That's right. She's wonderful. So, they offered it to Tim, and because nobody cared too much about the film, Tim and Paul Reubens had a pretty free hand. So, they were able to hire Danny Elfman and he wrote this unbelievable score. But, at the time, the executives and, later, the critics, thought it was horrible. They didn't like it. And, when *Pee-wee's Big Adventure* was released, not only the music but the whole movie was panned. It got really awful reviews.

MP: Really?

JG: Yeah, yeah. They said it was the worst movie ever made. Now, Tim Burton had signed a three-year contract with

Warner Bros. They always do that. If Warner's make a deal with a guy to direct a film, they make it for three films in case the first film is a hit. Because then the director's price will go up. But, while he's cheap, they can get three films from him at a low rate. And because he's eager to direct a movie, he will sign a deal like that.

But, the deal only commits the director, not the studio. They can drop the director whenever they want.

So, after these bad reviews came out, Warner's dropped him. They dropped his contract. And Tim was very depressed. He told me he went to Hawaii to try and get out of his depression.

So, they put the film out with the minimum of publicity, but it was a huge hit. The kids loved it. It was given a limited release, but per screen average was over 90%. It was practically full for every screening, and the cinema managers were saying: "This film is doing good business! We want to extend it for another week, and another week." And, so the head of distribution said: "We'd better release it a bit more – book it in more theaters." So, they expanded the release and they made a fortune. It was the second most successful movie that year for Warner Bros.

So, then they said: "Okay, Tim, we've changed our minds. We're re-upping your contract."

MP: Jesus, there are a lot of cliff-hangers in there!

JG: Always cliff-hangers. And so, they said: "Welcome back! You can make any film you want!"

MP: Hahaha! That must have been a surprise for him.

JG: Yeah, he really thought he'd never direct another film! But, now he could do anything he wanted. So, he hunted around and he found the script for *Beetlejuice*.

MP: Wow!

JG: And he made it and it was a hit as well – like *Pee-wee*, only more so. It grossed double what *Pee-wee* did.

MP: I love that movie.

JG: Yeah. So, he had one film left on his three-picture contract, and he started developing a story based on a character he'd drawn of a boy with scissors for hands. And he brought in the writer Caroline Thompson to do the screenplay. But Warner's put pressure on him to direct *Batman,* a project they'd been trying to get made for a long, long time.

MP: Hmm, hmm...

JG: At first, he didn't want to do it. But then he saw a graphic novel called *The Killing Joke*, and I think he was stimulated by the drawings of Brian Bolland, and he saw a way of doing it.

MP: They're kind of clever, to see, from his creativity, how he would make Batman really cool...

JG: Yeah, they like your creativity, but when you try to exercise it, they *don't* like it!

MP: What do you mean?

JG: Well, take the casting of Michael Keaton. Tim wanted Keaton to play Batman. And this was very contentious. Keaton was a skinny, comedy guy, and Batman's supposed to be buff and tough, and have a square jaw and a six-pack and muscles. He saves the day...

MP: Michael Keaton was so cool in it!

JG: Yeah, but everybody was like, "Shit! What's going on?" They were holding their heads. They thought *Batman* was gonna be the biggest bomb ever!

MP: Hahahaha!

JG: And Jack Nicholson, when Tim wanted him for the Joker, the studio said: "No, no, no! He's too old!" They thought the Joker was some skinny young guy with a manic laugh who wiggles a lot...

MP: When I think of this whole thing... These guys don't really have very good intentions. It's all self-interest. And they don't make it easy. But still, in the end, it worked out, didn't it?

JG: Well, yeah, you gotta give them credit for doing it. It was Bob Daly and Terry Semel. They were the co-presidents of Warner Bros. And *Batman* was their baby. Actually, they were both very nice guys. I met them, and spoke to them a few times. I liked them both. They were both charming diplomats. Essentially businessmen. I don't think they understood Tim, but who does? Hahaha! And there was a guy called Mark Canton. He was Head of Production. And these guys – Bob Daly, Terry Semel and Mark Canton – their heads were on the block. They hadn't had a hit in a while, and Mark Canton was a on five-year contract, which was coming up for renewal.

Everybody in town was predicting Mark Canton's downfall, and kind of salivating over it. They were telling each other *Batman* was going to be a disaster. And instead, it was the biggest hit in Warner Bros history. It made over $400 million. And Mark Canton was covered in glory! Hahahaha!

MP: Wow!

JG: So, after *Batman*, Tim's three-picture deal was up. So, they offered him another one. Same thing. "You can do any movie you want." So, he showed them *Edward Scissorhands*, and they said; "No. It's too weird."

MP: They wouldn't do it?

JG: No.

MP: Hahaha! After saying he could do any film he wanted?

JG: Right. So, he took it to Paramount. And they let him make it with an unknown actor in the lead – Johnny Depp. And it was a big hit.

MP: Wow!

JG: So, Warner Bros is going: "Oh shit!"

MP: "We gotta get Tim again?"

JG: Yeah. Specifically, to make a sequel to *Batman*, their biggest success ever. So, uh, then he did *Batman Returns*.

MP: So, what was Danny Elfman like on *Mars Attacks!*

JG: He was great. He called me up and asked what the music should be like, and I said: "Well it's gotta be sci-fi music. Spooky sci-fi music – but funny as well." We had a long talk about it. And he said: "Well, can you make me a tape of the kind of music you're talking about?"

So, I did that. And that was, that was kind of fun because I did a lot of research, and recorded nice bits of music from old sci-fi movies. Recorded them on my tape-recorder. And I put together three hours of music. Excerpts. Excerpts of a lot of different things. I remember that the theremin was a key instrument in many of those excerpts.

So, I gave Danny the tape and he said: "Oh, thank you very much." And, later on, he said it helped him a lot. Although, he didn't copy anything. Not at all. I didn't recognize anything from the tape in his film score. Although, the instrumentation, some of it, was similar.

He composed and recorded the *Mars Attacks!* score very quickly. He really is a marvel.

MP: Jesus Christ. That music was amazing. Just mind-blowing.

JG: It is mind-blowing, isn't it? And he did it in three weeks! I don't think he slept.

MP: Fuck!

JG: And he was conducting the orchestra and everything.

MP: He was also a trained conductor?

JG: Well, I don't know if he was trained, but he was telling the musicians what to do, and conducting them, and dashing around like a human tornado.

I remember, me, Tim and Lisa-Marie sitting in the booth and he was down in the studio, conducting the orchestra, and his energy was incredible. It was like his hair was on fire. And we all felt rather guilty, 'cause we were just sitting there, doing nothing. Just watching him, and eating marshmallows.

MP: Hahahaha!

JG: Haha! But you need this. Danny's an artist. Tim's an artist. Jack Nicholson's, an artist, Rod Steiger's an artist. We had a lot of artists on that film.

MP: Wow.

JG: That's why the movie turned out the way it did, I think. I mean, it could have been better. But, even with its flaws, it's a work of art, don't you agree?

MP: Oh yes!

JG: People said... A few people said later: "Oh, this is the world's most expensive B-movie."

MP: I think I read somewhere they called it a masterpiece.

JG: Well, I don't know about that.

MP: So, yeah. Let's talk about the role of the script. What is the role of the screenplay in a film? And what did *Mars Attacks!* mean to you?

JG: Well, the role of the script is… Essentially, it's a set of instructions. It's the plan of the movie. It's like a music score, or an architectural drawing. If you're composing music, you first do it in your head, then you write it down, and rewrite it, until you're satisfied with it. The same with architecture. You have ideas, then you draw them, and refine the drawings until they can be used for building a house.

In the case of *Mars Attacks!*, the initial disaster-movie idea came from Tim Burton, inspired by the little oil paintings on the baseball cards.

I watched some Irwin Allen disaster movies. *The Towering Inferno*, the *Poseidon Adventure* and *The Swarm*, which are all hilarious – especially *The Swarm*. And I found out that Irwin Allen made the first movie I ever saw in my life.

MP: What was that?

JG: *The Lost World*. I was eight years old. I used to walk home from school, and pass this movie theater – and I was attracted by the posters. I saved my pocket money and took my sister, who was six, to go see it. It was about a group of explorers in South America, who go down into this hidden valley, which is full of dinosaurs. We were terrified! My sister started crying so hard, I had to take her out!

So, disaster movies follow a formula. It's like if someone asked you to design a house, let's say, a Roman villa with an atrium. You have a basic architectural concept. A formula. So, you start with that. In the case of disaster movies, the formula is: different characters, from different walks of life, who you follow as they cope with the disaster. Lots of things happen. People get thrown together, some of them die, some of them fall in love, some of them resolve issues they have, and so on.

But knowing the formula is not enough. A movie needs to have a theme and a purpose. It's a big deal to ask people to pay money and give up two hours of their time to watch something. Time is our most precious commodity. It can't be replaced. So, you're under a sacred obligation to give them an experience that's worthwhile. And, for this, you need inspiration. So, when I started out, thinking about the story, I was repeatedly asking the universe: "What is this movie really about?" And the answer came back. "It's the world turned upside down."

Do you know about the Bacchanalia. Have you heard of it?

MP: Yes, wasn't that an orgy or something?

JG: Yes, in a way. The Bacchanalia, which was also called 'The World Turned Upside Down,' was a festival that happened in December. I think it started on the Winter Solstice – December 21st – and lasted for four days, which are the days when the sun seems to stop moving in the sky because all the days are of equal length. The World Turned Upside Down ended on the 25th, when the sun starts moving again and the days start getting longer.

MP: Oh, okay.

JG: And the way they celebrated this festival was amazing. Everybody switched ranks. So, the peasants would become aristocrats and the aristocrats would act like peasants. And there was no law. You could do anything and not be punished for it, which was where the orgies came in, and some of them were more like rapes.

You could do whatever you liked. Drink as much as you wanted. Beat up people you didn't like. Even rob people's houses. It was pandemonium.

I think it originated with the cult of Liber, who was similar to Bacchus or the Greek God Dionysus. Liber was the god of freedom. That's where we get the word 'liberty' from. And the Bacchanalia was popular and widely practiced throughout the Roman Empire until about 300 AD, when Christianity came in. After which it was suppressed and shortened and turned into Christmas.

Anyway, the purpose of the Bacchanalia was really as a safety valve. You know, under the oppressive social system of the Romans, which was really a slave system, tensions built up. So, everyone would release their pent-up tensions during the Bacchanalia. It was a way for society to let off steam.

So, why I'm giving you all this background is so you'll see how I came up with the *Mars Attacks!* story. I thought: "Okay. It's the world turned upside down." So, the peasants have to be kings and the kings are peasants. In other words, all the superior people in the movie, played by the movie stars, are thrown down, and the underdogs are raised up.

And this, I think, might be one reason why the movie has been popular for the past twenty-five years. I mean, of course, Tim's work is brilliant, and that's a lot of the reason but, underneath it all, watching the film is liberating. It makes you feel liberated. The authority figures are overthrown, and it's the forgotten people, the people who are not respected, who inherit the earth. Do you see what I mean?

MP: Yeah! It's like the revenge of the underdogs. Hahahaha! Though, hang on a minute, Tom Jones survives, and he's not an underdog, is he?

JG: No, but he's a musician.

MP: What, musicians don't count?

JG: Not if they're Tom Jones, they don't! They get a free pass! So, once I had that idea, I started sketching out the plot. And once I'd got that sorted out, I talked to Tim about it. And he liked it. He loved the idea of all the movie stars having dramatic death scenes.

MP: Hahahaha!

JG: So, you see I had to do a portrait of society. American society. And turn it upside down. And I was firing on all cylinders because, myself, I've always had a problem with authority. I had a difficult childhood, hated school and, when I left school, I couldn't bear being a wage-slave.

If it was 1381 now, I would join the Peasants' Revolt. The school history books don't tell the truth about that, by the way. It wasn't just a revolt by peasants from Kent. It was a nationwide revolution. And it wasn't only peasants, it was everybody.

The people wanted to end feudalism and set up a democracy. And they won. They defeated the king's forces and captured the king and then made him agree, and sign legal papers, to abolish the aristocracy, and share their land among the people, and have a democratically elected parliament.

But the rebel leaders were tricked and betrayed and then viciously persecuted for many decades afterwards. Every town in England had dissidents hung, drawn, and quartered.

So, in *Mars Attacks!* I indulged my fantasies, and the story was: the Martians attack, the establishment fails, and the most humble people in the story save the world.

And, when it came to depicting American society, well, I knew it pretty well. When I was ten years old, my father got a job in Scottsdale, Arizona, and we were there, the whole family, for about six months. I went to school there. It was great. I played baseball, learned about U.S. history, saluted the stars and stripes every day, and ate sloppy joes. I even had a pony in the school corral.

I loved grade school. It was much freer and more fun than a British elementary school. I loved America and didn't want to go back. And, after I grew up, I spent some time in New York, living with a friend in Hell's Kitchen. And I returned to NYC several times during the 80's, when my mother's play *Piaf* was done on Broadway in 1981, and in 1984, I think it was, when living in a flat in Manhattan writing a script for Malcolm McLaren, which was when I first met Lisa-Marie. And, in 1986, when I was helping my mother on a production of her play *Camille*.

And, in 1989, I moved to Los Angeles, and I'd been living and working there for five years before writing *Mars Attacks!*

So, I was no stranger to America and, of course, I'd been immersed in American culture all my life. My favorite TV show when I was a kid was *Rawhide*, starring Clint Eastwood. And my favorite reading matter was *Mad Magazine*, *Marvel Comics*, and *EC Comics*, like *Tales from the Crypt*.

But I was also a foreigner, an Englishman, an outsider. And, often, outsiders can see things that the locals don't see too well. I live in London, and I know London like the back of my hand, but when American visitors come over, they're always pointing out things I'd never noticed.

So, maybe that helped? Maybe I had an angle, or a perspective, on America that was a little different?

MP: It's almost eight o'clock. We should wrap this up.

JG: Okay.

MP: Is there anything else you'd like to say?

JG: No, I don't think so. Unless, maybe one thing. Do I sound to you like an expert?

MP: Well, yes. On this subject, yes.

JG: Then don't trust me!

MP: Hahaha!

JG: Do your own thinking, that's the thing. As Krishnamurti said: "Don't follow leaders." Be your own leader. And, what was that quote you told me from Suzuki Roshi?

MP: "In the beginner's mind there are many possibilities, but in the expert's mind there are few."

JG: That's it.

ACKNOWLEDGMENTS

Thanks to Universal Publishing for permission to quote lyrics from *Robin Hood* © Universal Publishing Group, Sony/ATV Music Publishing LLC, Warner Chappell.

Thanks to Anya Hastwell for line editing and style advice.

Thanks to Alex Billington at Tetragon Publishing for content design and typesetting.

For the use of his quote, "Only the impossible is worth doing," I'm grateful to Darma Arya Akong Tulku Rinpoche, the founder of ROKPA Trust, ROKPA International, and the Kagyu Samye Ling Monastery and Tibetan Center.

And my gratitude to Zen Master Shunryu Suzuki Roshi for his quote from *Zen Mind, Beginner's Mind*. "In the beginner's mind there are many possibilities, but in the expert's mind there are few."

INDEX

COMING SOON...

HOLLYWEIRD

By Jonathan Gems

Tales you've never heard before. Glamour, temptation, lust, greed, absurdity, and murder. Is truth stranger than fiction?

Jonathan Gems takes you on a laughter-filled VIP tour through the intestines of Hollywood, where dreams and nightmares really do come true.

CHAPTER 1

THE GREEN LIGHT

Okay, the year is 1990, and I'm in Los Angeles. My name, by the way, is Morris Adelman, lately of New York City, and I'm a playwright.

Let me start by saying that writing plays is no day at the beach. As well as the problem of coming up with good ideas, there are technical difficulties—like how to get your characters on and off stage, how to give them time to change their costumes, how to contrive the scene and lighting changes, and how to keep the action going, so it's not all just talk.

Constructing a play is no picnic either. It's like engineering a clock. Every cog, wheel, rivet, and tension bar has to be weighted, balanced, and sprung.

It generally took about six or seven months, working eight hours a day, for me to write a stage-play. And then, when it was done, I'd be faced with the monumental task of getting it put on.

For nine years, I wrote plays and struggled to get them produced with no help from my girlfriend, Pookie Eisnitz. For all those nine years, I lived in the same, roach-infested, one-room apartment on the Lower East Side, buying my clothes in thrift stores, and working at the filthy Hotel Duke so I could pay my bills. *False Gods* wasn't my first play—it was my fourth—but it was the first to strike gold. After many aborted starts, *False Gods* opened at the Minetta Lane Theater in the West Village.

The reviews were good, the show was sold out, and after it finished its run at the Minetta Lane, it transferred to The Circle in the Square.

A hit play is pretty much a miracle. If you are able to get a production, and are lucky with director, designer, and cast—and the public loves the play—it can still be crushed by the critics. And if there isn't enough publicity, nobody comes. Even if you get rave reviews and great publicity, the public can still stay away in droves if (1) there's another hit show they'd rather see, (2) the ticket prices are too high, (3) there's a power cut, (4) a terrorist alert, (5) a bus, train, or stagehand strike, (6) it's raining, or (7) there's no place to park near the theater.

When, in the spring of 1989, I was offered forty thousand dollars for the rights to *False Gods*, and another forty to turn it into a screenplay, I thought I was dreaming.

But I wasn't. It was real.

So, I broke up with Pookie Eisnitz, quit the Hotel Duke, and boarded American Airlines for my maiden flight to the Land of Dreams. I'd never written a screenplay before, but this didn't worry me too much because I'm a very determined individual. I can take a lot of punishment. I always have. It's one of the benefits of having an unhappy childhood.

When I got to L.A., I hit the ground running. The next day, I started a five-day course entitled: *Screenwriting—The Inside Scoop*. And, during my first week in Tinseltown, I read every page of the classic book *Screenplay* by Syd Field… twice.

And what I discovered was that, compared to writing plays, writing movies is a cinch. Here's an example. In a play, as I said, you have to devise plausible ways to get your characters on and off stage.

In the movies, you just write: "Cut to."

"Cut to: a snowstorm in Alaska."

How easy is that?

After I'd been in La La Land two weeks, all my views about theater had radically changed.

"The theater is archaic," I told Morgan Wacker, my new Hollywood agent.

I was in his swish fifth-floor office in the Creative Talent Management building on Wilshire Boulevard. Morgan Wacker, a genial man in his mid-forties, nodded in agreement. At least, I think it was agreement. It's hard to tell with him.

"Theater is a stagecoach," I announced, "and film is an automobile."

"And *False Gods*," he said, "is gonna be a fucking rocket."

I loved L.A. from the moment I saw it through the airplane window. Thousands and thousands of tiny houses, all with their own built-in swimming pools. Amazing. And, after I'd driven around West Hollywood, Bev Hills, and Santa Monica, I liked it even more.

The sunshine, the palm trees, the fairy-tale houses in every architectural style, the classy hotels and restaurants, the fancy stores, the beaches, the Pacific Ocean. What's not to like? Why were New Yorkers so crabby about it? The climate was perfect, the closets spacious, and the natives friendly.

Like Nat Greenberg.

Nat Greenberg was a writer with dark blond hair, bright white teeth, and a perfect tan. He looked like a surfer. (I later learned he often went surfing with his rabbi.)

Soon after meeting Nat, he invited me to his white clapboard house in Benedict Canyon, where I admired his pretty garden, and his pretty, actress girlfriend.

I first ran into Nat Greenberg at a screening at the Writers Guild of America (West).

"Are you Morris Adelman, the guy who wrote *False Gods*?" he said.

"Yes, I am," I said, flattered.

"That is *so cool!*"

I think I blushed. "Did you see it?"

"Uh-uhn." He shook his head. "Couldn't make it. But I heard all about it, and your play is *exactly* what I wanna do myself."

"Really?"

"Yeah, man. Theater is my dream."

Nat had a great reverence for playwrights, which was very gratifying, and he was a cornucopia of knowledge regarding the people and politics of the town. He knew who was who, and who wasn't who, and even who might be who in the future.

Nat had lived in L.A. for nine years, and written scripts for all the studios.

As I drove down Sunset Boulevard in my rental with the top down, I was in a state of grace. The gods had plucked me up and put me down in Movie Heaven. That old song 'Hooray for Hollywood' played in my head as I drove. I was going to write movies the whole world would see! I didn't care if I wrote rom-coms, action adventures, horror, sci-fi, or dog movies. I'd use them all to bequeath to the world my take on things.

And, as for the temptations that come with success, I'd spurn them! I wasn't going to turn into a coke-sniffing, girl-chasing degenerate. I'd be virtuous. I'd be valiant. I'd use my Writers Guild of America (West) card, and Syd Field's three-act screenplay structure, to spread the light and do good.

It took me only a week to find a perfect little bungalow in West Hollywood. It had two bedrooms with wallpaper depicting sage brush and cactus. Both bedrooms had ceiling fans. There was a Santa Fe-style living room with a B-movie fire, a bathroom with a rust-stained sink, and a bathtub decorated in seashells, and a kitchen shining with red and yellow tiles. I was going to live in the set of *I Love Lucy*!

Two days after moving into my little home, a car honked outside my window. It was my new pal, Nat Greenberg, in his silver-gray Toyota Land Cruiser. We'd arranged to play tennis with two of his buddies, and he'd come to pick me up.

I grabbed my brand-new tennis racquet, hoisted my gym bag, and rushed out the door.

It was a gloriously sunny day.

Gravel crunched under the tires of Nat's Land Cruiser as we pulled into the parking lot. The tennis club, surrounded by tall palm trees, took up several lots on Third Street, just west of La Brea. There were six hard-surface courts, and the club had a clubhouse with changing rooms, showers, a shop, and a café.

We played doubles: Nat Greenberg and I partnered against Zack and Floyd, two energetic guys in their late thirties, both screenwriters.

We played four sets. It was thirsty work.

When the match was over, we sauntered over to the air-conditioned clubhouse where, seated at a round wooden table, we drank fresh-squeezed orange juice, and the guys began talking about one of their friends.

"He's fucked," said Zack.

"I was mighty sad to hear about it," said Floyd, shaking his shaggy head.

"Yeah, it's a tough call," said Nat Greenberg. He looked over at me. "Buddy of ours," he explained. "Danny Fisher. You know him?"

"No, I don't."

"He's a writer."

"He was meant to be here today," said Zack, a tough guy with quiet eyes. "That's why Nat asked you along. To take his place."

"Oh. Did something happen to him?"

"Sure did," said Zack, ominously. "His script got green-lit."

"But isn't that good?" I was confused.

The three writers shook their heads.

"He oughtta be here, playing tennis," explained Floyd. "Instead, he's home slaving over rewrites."

Nat, seeing my perplexity, leaned forward on his elbows.

"Here's the thing, Morris," he said. "You don't want your scripts getting green-lit. I've been here, like, nine years, written a shitload of scripts, but, so far, touch wood…" He touched the leg of the table. "not a one of 'em's been made."

Zack and Floyd looked at him, nodding with satisfaction. I was more confused than ever.

Nat sipped his orange juice. "You're getting paid, right?"

"Excuse me?"

"For your script. *False Gods*. You're getting paid?"

"Yes, I am."

"That's good. So, when you're done, your agent will get you another assignment, and bump up your price."

"You'll get a bump," said Floyd.

"Usually about ten percent," said Zack.

"You're new, so you think this is a filmmaking industry," said Nat Greenberg. A lot of people think that when they first come out here. But Hollywood's not about filmmaking. It's about film *development*."

"That's right," said Floyd, nodding.

"Less than one percent of the scripts that get developed get made," said Nat. "How it works is the studios pay producers to develop scripts, okay? Some of the money goes to the writer, the rest goes to the producers and a whole crowd of other people."

"The town lives on development money," said Zack.

"That's right," said Floyd.

Nat nodded in agreement. "Producers, writers, directors, agents, managers, attorneys, accountants, some actors, all their wives, girlfriends, boyfriends, assistants, and babysitters buy their groceries, make their car payments, mortgage payments, and put their kids through school on development money."

"You can't make money out of movies," said Zack.

"If you wanna *lose* money," said Floyd, meaningfully, "make a movie."

Nat stretched out his legs. "The studios put out, what,

two hundred movies a year? How many of 'em are hits? Five? Six at the most."

"The rest of 'em bomb," stated Zack.

"That's right," said Floyd.

"And when a movie bombs," said Nat, "who gets the blame?"

"The writer," answered Zack.

"That's right," said Floyd.

"Sometimes they include the director," said Nat. "But they *always* blame the writer."

"The writer's the fall guy of choice," said Zack.

"Your phone stops ringing," said Nat.

"No more assignments," said Zack.

"I had a movie made once," said Floyd, pushing back his hair. "I didn't work for two years. Had to get a job at Staples. It was hell on earth."

The screenwriters fell silent.

Then Nat heaved a sigh. "Danny Fisher. It's too bad."

"Tough break," said Floyd.

"Rather him than us, though, huh?" said Nat.

"Makes you appreciate how lucky we are," said Floyd.

I gazed at my fellow screenwriters, all fit and tanned. They were experienced. They knew the ropes. They knew what they were talking about. Had I made a big booboo? Had I gone from the frying pan of New York into a fire of unproduced scripts in L.A?

For the first time since my arrival, I felt fear.

Maybe theater was a better bet after all?

ALSO FROM QUOTA BOOKS...

WHO KILLED BRITISH CINEMA?
by Jonathan Gems and Vinod Mahindru

REVIEWS

Who killed British cinema? It's a good question – especially since us Brits used to have the second biggest film industry in the world and now it is practically non-existent – and one that gets explored with real vigour in this interesting and well put-together book. It brings forth a mix of opinions whilst examining theories that could very well explain the 'death' of British cinema. Not only is it refreshingly honest, but it is also very detailed, as it is richly supported by intriguing stats and thought-provoking quotes from credible individuals from the film industry (taken from pre-arranged interviews). Because of this, there is real insight within the copy and, as it has been thoroughly researched, you can find out more about the history of British cinema and its unfortunate decline in a succinct way – you don't have to pore over lengthy textbooks or wordy theories to grasp the timeline of events. Overall, this makes for a riveting read that unpicks the political and cultural factors influencing media production and development over the decades, and if you are a film buff, you will particularly enjoy this in-depth piece of non-fiction. It even comes with a list of must-see British films!

HANNAH MONTGOMERY
www.whatson.guide
★★★★★ 5.0 out of 5 stars. **A Film Maker's Must Read!**

There is no shortage of resources for new and emerging film-makers; there are courses, free and paid; apps, some excellent and some not-so-good; there are many, many books written about every aspect of the art from writing the script to where to stay in Cannes when you're sending your new baby out into a world of adoring soon-to-be fans. All of these, to a greater or lesser degree, have their uses; but, if like me, you are involved in the production of shorts and / or features in the UK, there is one resource that will make you angry, very angry. A book (and documentary film) that will make your blood boil and, if you're anything like me, wonder why you decided to become involved in the obviously pointless world of UK film making in the first place. If it doesn't make you angry; if it doesn't make you want to scream in rage; if it doesn't make you say "This has ALL got to change" then you'd better go and do something else because, believe you me, you might think you love film and cinema, but you most certainly don't! The book "Who Killed British Cinema?" by Vinod Mahindru and Jonathan Gems, is an in-depth and comprehensive look at the British film industry – or rather, the lack of it – from its glory days when it was the second largest in the world to the present day where there is not one single British movie studio and 98% of the films in our cinemas are made by foreign entities. Now don't get me wrong, I'm certainly not a xenophobic Brexiteer Little Englander who thinks everything 'foreign' is bad; far from it. I'm a Remainer who has spent many years of his creative life in Europe, who loves the cinema of Bergman, Fassbinder (Rainer Werner rather than Michael) and Truffaut but who also grew up with, and has deeply rooted in his soul, the magnificent films of Michael Powell, Emeric Pressburger, Alberto Cavalcanti, Charles Crichton and David Lean – not to mention Terence Davies, Derek Jarman and Peter Greenaway.

Films that truly express our national identity, what it means to be British with all its peculiar sensibilities. Films that show our individualities and uniqueness in a way that the current diet of pap served up at the multiplexes could never hope to achieve. The book examines the way in which film funding has gone in this country, the role of such bodies as the BFI, BAFTA, the erstwhile Regional Screen Agencies, Creative England and, most interestingly the policy of successive governments, that have led to the demise of our most successful creative industry. Read it. Watch the documentary. Listen to what ex-CEO's of these august bodies say about spending 65% of their agency's budget not on film production but on admin and salaries. Read about funding bodies that fund production companies owned by members of the funding bodies who granted the funds in the first place. Do this and don't get mad, I dare you! This is not a negative book, nor a negative film. It is rather a call to arms for every filmmaker in the UK to say: "This is not right, this has to change." I found it inspirational. I found that, though my blood boiled at the sheer injustice of it all, it has increased my determination to succeed ten-fold. As Buckminster Fuller is quoted at the end of the documentary film: "You never change things by fighting the existing reality. To change something, build a new model that makes the existing model obsolete." If you buy one book about filmmaking, let it be this one. It will change your life and, who knows? maybe just help you to reinvent our beloved industry.

IAN MCLAUGHLIN MBKS

Q

www.quotabooks.com

info@quotabooks.com

Twitter: @Quotabooks